growing **STRONGER**

Press on in your encouraging, victorious book. Your story will be a great encouragement to multitudes. Yes, your battles you've fought through have made you strong and have given you great motivation and knowledge for your mission as Counselor.

—**Rita Bennett**, Marriage & Family Therapist, Litt.D., author of: *You Can Be Emotionally Free, EmotionallyFree.org.*

I used to believe that isolation was a good thing; it took a team of highly-skilled therapists at the Meier Clinic and a loving community of believers to convince me that connection with other safe, mature Christians promotes healing. I'm grateful that Mary Beth Woll and Dr. Paul Meier have written so clearly and powerfully! This book has reinforced key principles that encourage me to connect with Jesus to receive life, connect with others to pursue freedom, and pass on what I've learned to impact others.

—Meier Clinic client.

growing
STRONGER

*12 Guidelines
Designed to Turn
Your Darkest Hour
into Your
Greatest Victory*

MARY BETH WOLL, MA, LMHC
AND PAUL MEIER, MD

New York

growing STRONGER
12 Guidelines Designed to Turn
Your Darkest Hour into Your Greatest Victory

Published in New York, New York, by Morgan James Publishing. Morgan James and The Entrepreneurial Publisher are trademarks of Morgan James, LLC.
www.MorganJamesPublishing.com

The Morgan James Speakers Group can bring authors to your live event. For more information or to book an event visit The Morgan James Speakers Group at
www.TheMorganJamesSpeakersGroup.com.

A free eBook edition is available
with the purchase of this print book.

CLEARLY PRINT YOUR NAME ABOVE IN UPPER CASE

Instructions to claim your free eBook edition:
1. Download the BitLit app for Android or iOS
2. Write your name in **UPPER CASE** on the line
3. Use the BitLit app to submit a photo
4. Download your eBook to any device

ISBN 978-1-63047-510-9 paperback
ISBN 978-1-63047-511-6 eBook
Library of Congress Control Number:
2014921129

Cover Design by:
Rachel Lopez
www.r2cdesign.com

Interior Design by:
Bonnie Bushman
bonnie@caboodlegraphics.com

In an effort to support local communities and raise awareness and funds, Morgan James Publishing donates a percentage of all book sales for the life of each book to Habitat for Humanity Peninsula and Greater Williamsburg.

Get involved today, visit
www.MorganJamesBuilds.com

Peninsula and
Greater Williamsburg
Building Partner

DEDICATION

To Mary Beth's husband, Bob Woll, the best possible support when I was in crisis, and to our children, David, Bethany, Christa and Stevie, who, with God's help, also endured and grew strong in spite of or because of the trauma.

To Mom and Dad, Rev. John and Lola Baker, who trained me and my siblings, (John, Sue, and Joanna) for this race and gave me a wonderful, solid footing because of which I was able to rebound from trauma.

To my dear friend, Carmen Harris, to the incredible Prayer Group (June Munson, Peggy Hurd, Sandy Brannon, Mary Baffaro, Barbara Elder and Sheryl White), to Bible Study buddies Opal Oss and Lucie Buse, to Dr. Rita Bennett, and to Linda James, all of whom loved, taught, and prayed me through the healing process.

Special thanks to Paul Meier, MD, who shared the vision and writing of this book.

Many thanks to Dr. Jodi Detrick, who encouraged me to write the handbook for women in crisis (*Hundredfold*) from which this book originated. And thanks to Jane Etter and Alicia Adams who urged me to launch the first intensive-care support group (Snohomish Community Church) which has, as of this writing, already multiplied to three groups. Thanks also to Sherry Esp and Katie Saesan for their proofreading and editing expertise. And thanks to our Growing Stronger Prayer Partners, without whom this book could not have been written.

God's Word beautifully describes my gratitude for the God-honoring legacy left to me by previous generations of faithful family members, and also challenges me to pass on that legacy to future generations:

> I will open my mouth with a parable; I will utter hidden things, things from of old—things we have heard and known, things our ancestors have told us. We will not hide them from their descendants; we will tell the next generation the praiseworthy deeds of the LORD, His power, and the wonders He has done. He decreed statutes for Jacob and established the law in Israel, which He commanded our ancestors to teach their children, so the next generation would know them, even the children yet to be born, and they in turn would tell their children. Then they would put their trust in God and would not forget His deeds but would keep His commands (Psalm 78:2–7).

I pray that I will run the race God has set before me with all my might as I follow the pace set by my incredible, godly ancestors Rev. John and Lola Baker, Morrison and Gertrude Baker, James and Martha Baker, Vern and Esther Wellman, Rev. George and Lydia Armettie Andrews, and many Baker and Wellman aunts, uncles and cousins. I pray that I will faithfully pass the baton to our children and precious grandchildren: Liam Clay Woll, Oliver Duncan Woll, Rainier Andrew Frank, Lola Pearl Woll, June Flora Porter, and any grandchildren and great grandchildren "yet to be born."

TABLE OF CONTENTS

WELCOME TO GROWING STRONGER

The fact that you are reading this book indicates that either you have suffered a crisis or have a heart for helping hurting people. All of us experience times when we are hurting and need help. As a therapist (Mary Beth Woll, MA, LMHC) and a psychiatrist (Paul Meier, MD), we love helping people during those tough times and have devoted our careers to doing so. We love our jobs because it brings such great joy to help others. And that is obviously why you are here right now—learning to recover or to support others in their recovery—through Growing Stronger. No doubt you will also find camaraderie in this program with people of like mind and calling.

As the name "Growing Stronger" suggests, this ministry has a very definite purpose and goal—to help women in the church provide healing support for other women experiencing crises so that they can recover and return to a life of effectiveness for God and even become 30, 60, and 100 times more fruitful than before! (Mark 4:20).

The following pages offer a glimpse into the vision the Lord has given me (Mary Beth) as a result of years of counseling ministry and experiences of walking through my own times of crisis, trauma, suffering, and grief.

A number of years ago, I was attacked and nearly killed by a stranger. Even in those most frightening moments of my life, the Holy Spirit filled my heart in a militant, powerful way and comforted me with His presence which more than compensated for the nightmare I experienced.

Through God's miraculous intervention, I was able to escape. The attacker turned himself in to the police with a full confession and was sentenced to prison. After serving the criminal sentence, he was found by a jury to have a mental abnormality or personality disorder which made him highly likely to reoffend. He was civilly committed, indefinitely, as a sexually violent predator.

During the lengthy and agonizing process of recovering from the attack, I was reading through my prayer journal. I discovered an entry with a Scripture that God had impressed upon my heart just eleven days before the attack. "Fear will not come near you. Terror will be far from you. If anyone does attack you, it will not be My doing. Whoever attacks you will surrender to you" (Isaiah 54:14–15). At the time, I had thought in terms of a spiritual attack. Little did I know that God would deliver me from a physical attack and the assailant would surrender to me, just as the Scripture had said.

At first I was just so thrilled that God had saved my life and had given me back to my family and friends. Then post-traumatic stress set in. During these painful recovery times it was difficult, even with my resources as a counselor, to find the help I needed to navigate through these challenges. Although my dear husband Bob, loving family, friends, professionals, and ministries helped a lot, I often felt very much alone.

Through these experiences, God impressed upon me the need for the local church to provide a haven for women in such situations. Unfortunately, many churches are not prepared to offer this kind of support. Although nobody wants it to happen, women in crisis often fall through the cracks of the church structure. Sometimes church members don't know how to reach out, and the church staff may feel overwhelmed at the needs of women in crisis.

Though no one can totally escape the feelings of isolation which accompany suffering, participating in an ongoing, caring, healing group can go a long way toward easing that pain. In our national chain of Meier Clinics, we use small group therapy because it is so effective in bringing about rapid healing. Growing Stronger is designed to incorporate similar training, structure, and support to develop intensive-care-type groups in the local church that provide a safe haven for women going through those hurtful times we all eventually encounter.

The New Testament is filled with "ONE ANOTHER" concepts: Love one another, speak the truth in love to one another, exhort one another, and many others. In James 5:16, God promises that if we confess our "faults"—which includes our painful, "stuck" places—we will be healed. The Bible promises this, and research backs it up. Whether you have picked up this book because you need help in the midst of a crisis or you want to be better equipped to help women in crisis, we are grateful to God for people such as you!

May God bless you as you follow Him through this very important journey!

Mary Beth Woll, MA, LMHC
Therapist and Founder of Growing Stronger
Paul Meier, MD
Founder of the National Chain of Meier Clinics

GROWING STRONGER
GROUP LESSONS

Keep First Things First

Develop an intimate relationship with Jesus, the true Higher Power,
because you are powerless to overcome crises in your own strength, alone.

Chapter One

PREACH THE GOOD NEWS TO THE POOR

"The Spirit of the Sovereign Lord is on me, because
the Lord has anointed me to preach good news to the poor."
(Isaiah 61:1)

Keep First Things First

This beautiful scripture in Isaiah 61:1–4 describes Jesus' mission to those in need. Jesus read this passage aloud in the Synagogue, as recorded in Luke 4. His ministry, outlined in these verses, inspired Christian therapist Mary Beth Woll and Christian psychiatrist Paul Meier to write this book. Isaiah 61:1–4, along with Hebrews 12:1–13 and the Growing Stronger Guidelines that emerged from them, expresses the special love and passion we have to help women in crisis. Men are certainly welcome to study these teachings, but we wrote it specifically for women. We also have in mind those women who have successfully grown though their recent crises and want to return the favor by learning how to guide other women through the painful difficulties they may be experiencing. Together, we can bring meaningful solutions to women by preaching (NOT by being "preachy") the good news to the poor.

Who is "The Poor"?

While the term "poor" can refer to those in financial need, it also describes those who are poor in spirit—emotionally and spiritually— regardless of their financial status. This is the same word that Jesus used in the Sermon on the Mount when He said, "Blessed are the poor in spirit, for theirs is the Kingdom of Heaven" (Matt. 5:3). The "Kingdom of Heaven" not only refers to that eternal and perfect place where God exists, but a new life that begins now when we turn ourselves over to God. We all come to a point when we realize that we have a need and are powerless to meet it in our own strength—in other words, we are poor in spirit. That is when we are most ready to receive the Gospel—the Good News—and ask Jesus to help us! He hears our cry for help and opens the way to new and wonderful possibilities. We begin to live His way by His power working in and through us.

See One, Do One, Teach One.

In my (Dr. Meier's) latter years of medical school, during our clinical studies, we were taught a simple rule of thumb: "See one, Do one, Teach one." When I learned to deliver babies, for example, I watched a skilled Ob-Gyn, MD deliver babies, including some complicated cases. Then it was my turn to deliver twenty-two babies myself. What an exciting delight it was to witness the miracle of life firsthand! Then I was encouraged to help fearful medical students who had been trained but had not yet delivered their first baby.

The same principle applies to you, the readers of this book. We trust you will SEE how to overcome crises. We firmly believe most of you will use the information you glean from this book to DO the Twelve Growing Stronger Guidelines presented in these pages. When you feel relief from your crises, we hope you will empathetically TEACH these solutions to other women you love. Some of you will do this on an individual-to-individual basis, while others will be inspired to start Growing Stronger Groups, another goal of the authors. We hope these groups pop up all over America, and other countries as well, thus helping thousands of women.

From time to time, we all face struggles and feel "poor" in spirit. The authors of this book have certainly struggled through plenty of crises ourselves over the decades. We have developed these Twelve Growing Stronger Guidelines as a result of discovering what worked in our own lives as well as the lives of many hundreds of our clients. The purpose of Growing Stronger Groups is to bring healing to wounded women so they can recover and become stronger and more productive than ever before. But how can they heal and become all they were created to be without the Great Physician, Jesus? We want to reach out with love and acceptance to all who come, whether believers or not. But introducing them to Jesus is the greatest gift we can offer!

First Things First

Some of you in our reading family already know Jesus personally and are seeking to develop a deeper level of intimacy with Him. You need His wisdom and strength to get through your current crises and grow stronger in the process. Others of you have never prayed to Jesus to become the Savior and Lord of your life. Still others already have a close relationship with Jesus but have never known how to guide someone else to put her trust in Jesus personally. Wherever you are in this spiritual journey, we would all do well to follow the example of Jesus' ministry and give the Gospel first priority. When we have Jesus, we have, potentially, all we need. Romans 8:32 reminds us, "He who did not spare His own Son, but gave Him up for us all—how will He not also, along with Him, graciously give us all things?"

When Jesus began His ministry by teaching in the synagogues and preaching, "The kingdom of God is near. Repent and believe the good news" (Mark 1:15), there were many who came to Jesus not knowing who He was or what He was preaching. They simply came because they or their loved one had a need and wanted to be healed. Some women will come to Growing Stronger Groups in the same way, not really knowing Jesus, but needing support. With this in mind, Growing Stronger Groups build bonds by showing love, compassion, and concern while prayerfully looking for every opportunity to share the Gospel in personal ways. We don't begin meetings with a sermon, but express the love of Jesus through meaningful, caring relationships, often sharing with each other what we have learned—sometimes the hard way!

When we share God's love in this way, He is caring for our needs through each other. He could do it all by Himself if He wanted to, but He doesn't want to! He loves to work in teamwork with us. He wants us to be His "Living Epistles." In a multitude of counselors—not just professionals, of course—there is safety (Proverbs 11:14). God loves to use people to love and help other people. The Apostle James (in James 5:16) taught us a principle we have used in the Meier Clinics national chain to heal many thousands of people for many years: "Confess your faults one to another, and pray one for another, that (you) may be healed" (KJV). Also, confessing to others about crises that are not our fault can help us heal within these loving relationships.

Here-and-Now Help with Heaven's Perspective

It is important to remember that if we help people through life crises yet neglect to explain how they can know God personally, we have only given them temporary assistance with transitory needs. Eternity is a very long time. The worst crisis of all is to be forever separated from the God who made us. If you were to meet someone who is struggling financially, you could either bring that person a fish daily, or teach her HOW TO FISH so she could learn to care for herself in the future. Even better, you could bring her some fish to eat while she is learning to use the new fishing pole you just gave her!

The same principle applies to helping women in crisis. We can teach specific solutions, potentially making others dependent on us to think for them. Or we can introduce them to Jesus who will then guide and assist them in applying these basic guidelines, leading them into even deeper solutions in their lives.

Matthew 6:33 says, "Seek first His kingdom, and His righteousness, and all these things will be given to you as well." As we put Jesus first, He cares for our needs. This does not mean, of course, that when we become Christians, all our problems will be solved. Salvation is instantaneous, but sanctification, the process of becoming more like Jesus, is life-long. God never runs out of things to work on in our lives, no matter how mature we are physically, emotionally, or spiritually. But God Himself is the ultimate source of answers to our earthly and eternal concerns.

Relief from crises and the comfort of earthly things may satisfy in the short term, but Jesus is eternally satisfying. In John 4, Jesus said to the woman at the well, "Everyone who drinks this water will be thirsty again, but whoever drinks the water I give him will never thirst" (John 4:13). Not only is His refreshment everlasting, it is a fantastic renewable inner resource to meet the soul's thirst now—and forever. "Indeed, the water I give him will become in him a spring of water welling up to eternal life" (John 4:14).

So, How Do We Do That?

You may say, "I agree. We need God, above all. But how does one even begin a relationship with Him?" One easy-to-memorize way to enter into a personal relationship with Jesus, or to introduce people to Jesus is called, "The Romans Road." Anyone can start on this life-changing journey with Him by understanding and acting on these basic biblical truths:

- **We are all sinners in need of a Savior.** Romans 3:23 says, "For all have sinned and fall short of the glory of God."
- **Without Jesus, we are separated from God, now and in the afterlife.** Romans 6:23a says, "For the wages of sin is death..."
- **But with Jesus, we can have eternal life, beginning right now.** Romans 6:23b says, "...but the gift of God is eternal life in Christ Jesus our Lord."

So what must one do to have this eternal life with Jesus? Romans 10:9–10 explains, "That if you confess with your mouth, 'Jesus is Lord,' and believe in your heart that God raised Him from the dead, you will be saved. For it is with your heart that you believe and are justified, and it is with your mouth that you confess and are saved." Trust God to forgive your sins and enter your life. He is offering this to you as a free gift, not as a result of anything that you can do to earn it. As Ephesians 2:8–9 says, eternal salvation is a result of God's grace through faith in Him, not your own good works, like most religions erroneously teach. If your good works could save you, then you would really have something to boast about. But the truth is that we are saved by faith in Jesus alone. As a result, good works flow from a heart that has been made brand new.

Personal Testimony

I (Dr. Meier) learned this Romans Road when I was a teen and used it to win a few friends to Jesus, but I was fairly shy. As a 19-year-old freshman in college during the Vietnam War, I decided to spend my Saturdays at a "Servicemen's Center" where I would help to provide free food, play ping pong or other games, or just sit and talk with servicemen in training before they were shipped to Vietnam.

My first time there, I was scared to death to witness to a soldier—to any soldier at all. I stood by the front door outside the building in a downtown area, having never even gone in yet, and prayed silently, "Dear God, please make the first one easy."

As I was praying silently, standing there on the sidewalk, I felt someone tapping me on the back. I turned around, and to my surprise, it was a soldier. A complete stranger to me, he said, "By any chance, are you a Christian, and can you show me how to become one? I got a letter from my mom last night and she said she is praying I will become a Christian before I risk my life in Vietnam."

I escorted him up the stairs (the first time for both of us), showed him Romans 3:23 and 6:23 and assisted him to pray for Jesus to forgive him and enter his life. He had great joy, but so did I! The others were not that easy, but the Lord used my willingness and time those Saturdays to lead about 300 soldiers to Christ. Only God knows how many of them met the Lord in Heaven during the war. God blessed my willingness to produce fruit, in spite of my fears.

The Gospel Grows.

Sometimes, we plant a seed of the Gospel in a person's life and someone else comes later to harvest it. Other times, our role is to water the seed previously planted by showing kindness to people for Jesus's sake. In John 4:35–38, Jesus said:

> Behold, I say to you, lift up your eyes and look at the fields, for they are already white for harvest. He who reaps receives wages, and gathers fruit for eternal life, that both he who sows and he who reaps may rejoice together. For in this the saying is true: 'One sows and another reaps.' I have sent you to reap that for which you have not labored; others have labored, and you have entered into their labors.

Growing Stronger Groups welcome women in all stages of spiritual growth, and through compassionate, loving help, share the Good News that Jesus has the answers.

Discussion Questions

1. Have you ever received Jesus as your Savior? If so, please share that experience with the group. Some know they have done so, but do not remember the specific moment when they asked Jesus into their hearts and lives. Others experienced a distinct encounter with God when they first trusted Jesus.

   Dr. Meier trusted Jesus in his Sunday School class when he was six years old, but rededicated his life in a more intimate way at age 16 after two dramatic dreams one night.

   At age 5, Mary Beth tearfully confessed to her mother that she had lied to her about something. Her mother forgave her and then wisely reminded, "There's someone else you need to tell that you are sorry: God." Then she led Mary Beth in a prayer to ask Jesus to forgive her and to come in to her heart. As Mary Beth grew, so did her faith in God and deep personal relationship with Him.

Everyone's moment of introduction to Jesus as Lord and Savior is unique, so we hope you will share your own personal experience with others.

_____

_____

_____

_____

_____

_____

2. If you have not yet received Christ, would you describe yourself as (a) still contemplating the decision, (b) having some questions about receiving Christ, or (c) not yet ready at this time?

_____

_____

_____

_____

_____

_____

3. If you replied to the previous question with answer "a" or "b," your group leader will be happy to discuss any questions you may have.

As with any big decision, it is wise to get counsel. Our leaders are experienced in this area and will be glad to help. If you are not in a group, but are reading this book and would like to know Jesus personally right now, then sincerely pray this sample prayer:

Dear Jesus,

You and I both know that I have committed sins in my life—done things at times that have hurt others. I believe You died on the cross and rose to life again to pay for my sins. I ask You right now to come into my heart and become the Lord of my life. Forgive me for the sins I have committed in the past or may commit in the future.

Amen.

Chapter Two

BIND UP THE BROKENHEARTED

"The Spirit of the Sovereign Lord is on me…
He has sent me to bind up the brokenhearted."
(Isaiah 61:1)

Beginning the Healing Process

In medical school, we learned that if you break your arm and it heals properly, that part of your arm will be stronger than the rest of it. If you were to break that arm again in a future accident, it would not break where it had previously healed. In the same way, a broken heart can be painful. Nearly all of us have felt this ache at one time or another, but as God heals our broken hearts, He makes us stronger in the end than we ever were before.

Don't Suffer Alone.

After Growing Stronger Guideline #1 (establishing an intimate relationship with Jesus as the one, true Higher Power), we move on, out of our loneliness, to Growing Stronger Guideline #2. Here, we bring and discuss our broken hearts, in the presence of God, with His loving people, our spiritual brothers and sisters. We can entrust our aching souls to a friend, close relative, pastoral counselor, professional counselor, Christian psychiatrist or psychologist, or a Growing Stronger Group, if there is one in your area. Celebrate Recovery groups are also very helpful if you can find one at a church near you.

A shared burden becomes a half burden. Simply telling your story to God and one or more caring persons will likely relieve a great deal of your pain. And that is only the beginning, as someone with a healed heart often responds by passing on to others the renewal that they have received. But healing is a process, as reflected in the Twelve Growing Stronger Guidelines. The first two guidelines are the most important and necessary steps. First trust Jesus for love, support, and guidance; then take your broken heart and burdens to Him and significant others.

As you begin to recover, 1 Peter 5:10 tells us that God will "personally come and pick you up, and set you firmly in place, and make you stronger than ever" (TLB). It is this passage of Scripture that inspired the name of this book and the groups we hope will spring from it: Growing Stronger!

Jesus Heals Broken Hearts.

Jesus considers mending broken hearts to be critical, second only to preaching the Gospel. In fact, Jesus said that the whole Law can be summed up in two commands: first, "Love the Lord your God with all your heart and with all your soul and with all your strength and with all your mind," and second, "Love your neighbor as yourself" (Luke 10:27). To illustrate loving our neighbor, Jesus tells the parable of the Good Samaritan (Luke 10:25–37). Here we are given an example which instructs us in the heart-mending ministry. Let's look at this story together and reflect on the actions of this compassionate man who encountered a stranger in need. What did he do that the others did not, and how can we learn from him?

He Took Pity on Him.

The Good Samaritan saw the state of the wounded man and, unlike the priest and the Levite who passed by on the other side of the road, he felt sympathy for him. The Samaritan already had plans for that day. Like the others, he was en route from Jerusalem to Jericho. He wasn't out looking for an opportunity to do good deeds. He simply came upon the wounded man in the course of his travels. But the Good Samaritan was moved with compassion.

Sometimes, what seems to be a detour, or even an interruption, in our day can turn out to be the greatest blessing to others. A good friend and mentor to Mary Beth, Vivian Smith, used to say, "A Christian can do more good 'by accident' than others can do on purpose!" What may seem like a chance encounter, however, may be just what the Lord had planned. As Psalm 37:23 says, "The steps of a good man are ordered by the Lord, and He delights in his way." And, again, in Proverbs 16:9, "A man's heart plans his way, but the Lord directs his steps" (NKJV).

He Went to Him.

The Samaritan allowed his compassion to move him to action. He didn't just feel badly about the man's condition. He responded to the urging in his heart and DID something!

This is also the mission of Growing Stronger—to help women in crisis who might otherwise be overlooked. Whether it is a physical or emotional need, well-wishes are not enough. James 2:8 encourages, "If you really keep the royal law found in Scripture, 'Love your neighbor as yourself,' you are doing right." Helping those in need is a true expression of our faith in Jesus. If we have faith but no action to back it up, the Bible says that "faith by itself, if it is not accompanied by action, is dead" (James 2:17).

He Bandaged His Wounds.

Sometimes, applying a bandage—like a tourniquet to stop the bleeding—can be the first step toward healing and preventing infection.

In the heart-mending ministry, the first step toward "stopping the bleeding" may mean listening to a sister's story of trauma and holding her while she cries. It may even include encouraging her to remove herself from a dangerous situation long enough to stabilize and strategize about the next steps in the healing process.

He Poured Oil and Wine into the Wound.

Oil and wine, sort of an ancient first aid kit, supplied soothing and antiseptic properties. In binding up the broken hearted, we apply the "oil" of grace which soothes the soul and prepares the listener for the "wine"—the antiseptic of truth. Like Jesus, we need to be "full of grace and truth" (John 1:14) as we carefully dress their wounds. Our loving words and actions must be based in truth or they will not bring the necessary healing.

He Put the Man on His Own Donkey.

The injured man had no strength to help himself. When the Samaritan put him on his own donkey, he was offering his personal resources to someone who, for the moment, had none.

In times of crisis, even ordinary, daily activities can become overwhelming. Following the example of the Good Samaritan, we can offer our shoulder to help carry the burdens of those who have temporarily lost their own strength.

He Took Him to an Inn.

The wounded man needed to get off the dangerous road and into a safe place where he could recuperate.

Similarly, people in crisis may need a shelter, a haven, in which they can recover. For some, the "safe place" might, simply, be a listening ear. Others may actually need to change their living situation in order to be out of danger. Note that the Good Samaritan did not take the man into his own home, which was too far North for this wounded man to travel. He found a resource designed for that purpose. While it is important to practice hospitality, we must also remember to maintain personal boundaries for safety reasons, as well as to avoid burnout.

He Took Care of Him.

The Bible says that the Good Samaritan took care of the wounded man and stayed with him until the following day. He supported him through the life-threatening period, then he turned him over to the care of the innkeeper.

There are times when crises can be disabling to those experiencing them. At such times, they will need critical social, emotional, and spiritual care that they cannot provide for themselves.

He Gave Sacrificially.

He gave the innkeeper two silver coins and offered to reimburse him for other expenses. The Good Samaritan gave generously and responsibly from his own resources to help the wounded man. The two silver coins were a good-faith down payment toward the rest of his care which involved food, lodging, and recuperation needs. These large silver coins were called "denaria." Each coin equaled approximately a day's wage for the average worker at the time. Apparently, the Samaritan had not only enough money for his own needs but a surplus to help others, as well.

Ministering to others requires us to give of ourselves. Sometimes, we even give sacrificially, knowing that "He who is kind to the poor lends to the Lord, and He will reward him for what he has done" (Proverbs 19:17). Just like the disciples who, through the miracle of the five loaves and two fish fed over 5,000 people with twelve basketsful leftover, we too can live this life of generosity and bring glory to God as He promises to replenish our supply. 2 Corinthians 9:10–11 promises that "He who supplies seed to the sower and bread for food will also supply and increase your store of seed and will enlarge the harvest of your righteousness. You will be enriched in every way so that you can be generous on every occasion, and, through us your generosity will result in thanksgiving to God."

He Delegated Responsibility.

He asked the innkeeper to care for the wounded man until he returned. After attending to the immediate crisis, the Good Samaritan went on to conduct his own business. He didn't neglect his personal life and responsibilities, nor did he expect to do everything himself, but understanding his limitations, he made arrangements for others to help with the man's care.

As we reach out to women in need, it is important to remember that each person in the group provides a part of the solution as we relate to each other in love. No one person can do it all. We have our limitations too, and we need each other. Romans 12:27 reminds, "Now you are the body of Christ and each one of you is a part of it"! We are not the Savior. Only Jesus is able to fill that job description!

The Wounded Man did not Stay at the Inn.

The story implies that the wounded man eventually recovered and left the inn to return to his normal life.

The whole point of bearing one another's burdens is to come alongside each other during those times when we are not able to bear it alone. But after the season of recovery, we will return to a life of fruitfulness, stronger than ever before.

Avril VanderMerwe, professor at Seattle Bible College, often tells of growing up near a gold mine in South Africa. She frequently enjoyed the visitors' center at the mine where they demonstrated the crushing and melting methods used in the long gold refining process. The end product was a solid gold brick! Visitors were invited to come up and handle the brick. They challenged any strong man in the audience to attempt to pick it up. If anyone could pick up the brick with one hand, it would be his to keep. No one was ever able to meet that challenge (VanderMerwe forthcoming),

In the same way, though our distressing circumstances may seem very heavy, and at times more than we can bear, the Bible refers to them as "our light and momentary troubles." Like the pure gold that comes from much refining, these burdensome trials "are achieving for us an eternal glory that far outweighs them all" (2 Corinthians 4:17)!

Words of Wisdom for Helpers

Finally, consider another element involved in this parable. While the Samaritan played a critical role in saving the life of the wounded man, he did not do it all himself. He had help from the innkeeper—and the donkey! Whether it is our turn to help others, or if we are currently the one in need, rest assured that God has people and methods to provide for those needs.

In Proverbs 4:7, God encourages us to "Get wisdom." One critical way to get wisdom is to learn from our own hurts and healing so that we are better able to empathize and bring healing to others. The wounds of our past do not disqualify us. In fact, they empower us if we have worked through them. From the world's point of view, I (Dr. Meier) have had lots of success in this life. But God knows the wounds I have suffered from time to time. Yet, I thank God even for these wounds because they help me learn to protect myself and make me better able to help others along the way.

Discussion Questions

1. Sometimes crises can "ambush" us, as in the case of the wounded man, in such a way that we are not even able to ask for help. In such times of need, we must rely on the strength and goodness of others. Have you ever experienced such a time? How did others help you?

_____

_____

_____

_____

_____

_____

2. Other times, we are able to ask for help, although it may be difficult to do so. Read Galatians 6:2–5. When are others to help us carry our burdens, and when are we to carry our own load?

These verses sound contradictory in English versions of the Bible. In one verse we are told to bear our own burdens. In another verse of the very same passage, we are told to bear each other's burdens to fulfill the law of Christ. A contradiction? No. In the original Greek, these verses are much more understandable. What they are saying is that we should all bear our normal emotional loads. We should not depend on others for things we are fully capable of handling ourselves. Instead, we should bear each other's "overburdens" to fulfill the law of Christ.

If you were going with friends on a camping trip, you would each carry your own backpack. It would be considered lazy and dependent to expect someone else to carry her backpack and yours as well, but the camp cook may need to carry the extra weight of pots and pans. In that case, the rest of the group should pitch in to help carry her overload and fulfill the law of Christ.

When you come to a friend with your broken spirit and overwhelming burden, you are doing the right thing! You are also giving others the wonderful experience of helping you heal and grow emotionally and spiritually. When you become strong, you will be delighted to bear the overburdens of others as well. Many will want to reach out, possibly even starting a Growing Stronger Group in their area. Then they can share support with others who also need the benefit of the Twelve Growing Stronger Guidelines.

_____

_____

_____

_____

3. Each one of us could easily play the part of any person in the parable. With which of these people do you most identify right now and why?

_____

_____

_____

_____

4. The responses of the priest and Levite seem surprising, given that they were "in the ministry" of their day. The reality is that, like the Good Samaritan, all Christians are called to minister in a Christ-like manner to needs that God brings our way. What kind of ministry opportunities have come along your path?

_____

_____

_____

_____

_____

5. Which of the above steps come most naturally to you as you relate to others in need? Which are more of a challenge and why?

_____

_____

_____

_____

6. How did Jesus model boundaries in ministry?

Consider Luke 4:42, Luke 6:1–10, Luke 9:10, 11, 18, 28, and Luke 11:1–4. Discuss these passages, one by one, with your "overburden bearer" or with the sister you are helping with her overburden.

_____

_____

_____

_____

_____

7. An important part of successful living involves a continual review of priorities, which help define our boundaries. How are the boundaries in your life right now? (See the Bibliography for help in this area.)

An example of poor boundaries is when you are suffering alone and not sharing your overburden with God and others. Another example is when you are feeling overwhelmed as a result of being overly obligated for the burdens of others. This happens when you carry others' normal emotional load instead of saying the "NO" word and allowing them to shoulder their rightful responsibilities.

God doesn't want you to be a masochist. He doesn't want you to be an enabler who earns the money, for example, to support the drinking habits of an alcoholic mate or significant other. That is called CODEPENDENCY. If codependency is your problem, we recommend you read _Love is a Choice_ by one of the authors of this book, Paul Meier, MD, and his associates (Meier, MD, Paul D.; Hemfelt, Dr. Robert; Minirth, MD, Frank B. 1989). In 1993, Dr. Meier appeared on The Oprah Winfrey Show to present this book. It sold well over a million copies and is still helping thousands of people around the world to identify and overcome the enormous problem of codependency.

_____

_____

_____

_____

8. This parable says that the injured man was "half dead." He may have been too weak to even notice what the Good Samaritan was doing for him. The Samaritan did the right thing even though he got no response from the person he was helping. Sometimes ministering to others can be a thankless job, but as we do it "for the least of these," we are doing it for Jesus (Matt. 25:40). What are some areas of your life where you do things for Jesus in this way?

_____

_____

_____

_____

9. At the end of the parable, Jesus tells us, "Go and do likewise" (Luke 10:37). There is a time to receive ministry from others and a time to give as well. Describe when you, or someone you love, have been "the brokenhearted." Describe when you have been the one who came alongside to help.

_____

_____

_____

_____

Confession Leads to Freedom

To become truly free from bondage and truly healed, you must confess your own sins and flaws to safe, significant others as well as to Jesus.

Chapter Three

PROCLAIM FREEDOM FOR THE CAPTIVES

"The Spirit of the Sovereign Lord is on me ... to proclaim freedom for the captives and release from darkness for the prisoners."
(Isaiah 61:1)

Jesus has come to proclaim freedom for the captives and a release from darkness for the prisoners! What wonderful news! But what exactly does it mean to be free because of Jesus?

Freedom from Sin

Sin is a trap. At first, sin looks good, but if we allow ourselves to be drawn into temptation and indulge, like the proverbial moth to the flame, we are injured. Jesus frees us from the bondage of sin by paying the penalty for our sin and forgiving us for the wrongs we have committed. Then He gives us His Holy Spirit to live inside us. The Holy Spirit helps us to live for Him as we turn away from what our human nature desires and set our minds on what the Spirit desires.

All sin hurts someone. We don't really want to go through life hurting ourselves, others, or even God, who grieves when we sin. Jesus taught us many "one another" concepts in Scripture. He taught us to love one another, speak the truth in love to each other, exhort one another, and express anger to each other without getting vengeance. He also taught us to confess our faults to one another (as we have seen in James 5:16), to forgive each other from the heart, and to restore each other gently if we do fall into sin's trap.

Recently, when Mary Beth was driving with her two grandsons, Liam (6) and Oliver (3 ½), they passed a local casino. The grounds were beautifully decorated with many lighted evergreen trees. She exclaimed, "Look at the beautiful Christmas trees!"

Liam quickly warned, "It's a trap, Nonny! People think it's so beautiful, but they don't know that if they go inside, they might get hurt!" Then, he wistfully added, "But it really is beautiful, isn't it, Nonny?"

Such a smart boy!

This inspired a wonderful discussion of good and evil, bad guys and good guys, the traps of temptation that the devil sets for people, and how Jesus died for us so that we could be forgiven and set free from sin.

Little Oliver concluded, "When God turns bad guys into good guys, then the bad guys will be free!"

"That's right, Ollie!!! You got it!"

From the mouths of babes!

What these precious little boys don't know, yet, is that we are all "bad guys" who need to be turned into "good guys" through Jesus! As we have often heard, "Sin will take you farther than you want to go, keep you longer than you want to stay, and cost you more than you want to pay" (Source unknown). As Romans 3:23 states, "ALL have sinned and come short of the glory of God." In our own power, we can't "turn ourselves into good guys" because, as Jesus said, "Everyone who sins is a slave to sin" (John 8:34).

Fortunately, Jesus doesn't leave us hopelessly captive, but goes on to say in the very next verse, "Now a slave has no permanent place in the family, but a son belongs to it forever. So if the Son sets you free, you will be free indeed."

Helping Others to Freedom

Sometimes people need others to help them see the way to freedom. One of the greatest blessings in life is to help fellow human beings find relief from pain and discover love and joy again. When that happens, they naturally want to help others—often their own friends and relatives—to find freedom as well. In the counseling ministry, there is a wonderful ripple effect as the person seated across the room may influence countless others, potentially changing the very outcome of their lives, as well as the lives of generations that follow! We see this every day at Meier Clinics as referrals come from clients or former clients who overcame their struggles.

Harriet Tubman is a great example of this type of ripple effect. A devout Christian and hero from the pre-Civil War days, Harriet was personally responsible for leading hundreds of American slaves to freedom. Born into slavery around 1820 (she did not know her exact date of birth), Harriet escaped in 1849 and returned many times to rescue family members and others who were not yet free. She developed what was called "The Underground Railroad," an elaborate system of secret safe houses organized to smuggle slaves from the South to freedom in the North (Harriet Tubman Biography n.d.).

Before her escape, Harriet said, "I had reasoned this out in my mind: there was one of two things I had a right to, liberty or death; if I could not have one, I would have the other" (Tubman). She later described her experience of escaping slavery as glorious! "When I found I had crossed that line, I looked at my hands to see if I was the same person. There was such a glory over everything; the sun came like gold through the trees and over the fields, and I felt like I was in Heaven" (Tubman).

But enjoying this freedom was not enough for Harriet. She was alone in this free land and wanted to share it with others. "I had crossed the line of which I had so long been dreaming. I was free, but there was no one to welcome me to the land of freedom; I was a stranger in a strange land" (Tubman).

Though she was not physically strong, having suffered permanent damage from severe beatings and abuse as a slave, Harriet was courageous and indomitable. This modern-day Moses endured severe perils and hardships to bring others to freedom. William H. Seward said of her, "I have known her long, and a nobler, higher spirit, or a truer, seldom dwells in the human form" (Tubman).

In bringing many slaves to freedom, Harriet bravely vowed:
But to this solemn resolution I came: I was free, and they should be free also; I would make a home for them in the North,

and the Lord helping me, I would bring them all there. Oh, how I prayed then, lying all alone on de cold, damp ground. 'Oh, dear Lord,' I said, 'I ain't got no friend but You. Come to my help, Lord, for I'm in trouble! (Tubman).

And help He did, indeed, as she led hundreds of slaves to freedom. Harriet rejoiced in this victory when she said, "I was the conductor of the Underground Railroad for eight years, and I can say what most conductors can't say; I never ran my train off the track and I never lost a passenger" (Tubman).

Soul Freedom

Surprisingly, there were some American slaves who chose to remain in bondage. In a similar way, it is possible for us to be free from sin in our spirits while our soul area (the mind, the will, and the emotions) still carries baggage. Whether we are brand new Christians or have been Christians for a while, we all, from time to time, need freedom from harmful habits and mistaken mindsets.

We see an example of this in John chapter 11, where we read the story of Lazarus, whom Jesus raised from the dead. Even though Lazarus was brought back to life by the mighty Word of the Son of God, he came out of the tomb still wrapped in grave clothes. He had to have someone take off the grave clothes with which he was bound before he could walk into his new life unhindered.

He Does His Part, We Do Our Part.

Couldn't Jesus have blasted off those old grave clothes when He raised Lazarus from the dead? After all, Lazarus had been dead four days, and Jesus brought him back to life! In contrast, what are a few strips of linen? Notice here that Jesus told someone else to take off the grave clothes. Lazarus was alive, but he wasn't free! Jesus chose to allow those who witnessed this miracle to take part in Lazarus' return to complete participation in life!

Since we, as the Body of Christ on the earth, are now called to do the works of Jesus, we can also proclaim freedom to the captives. Like Lazarus, we need each other, empowered by Christ, to help us in our path to freedom. God has provided a place for all of us to belong and be free—the Body of Christ! As each member does its part, and each person is willing to give and receive help, liberty will be ours!

We like to ask our clients sometimes, "If you were lost at sea in a rowboat, and finally saw shore in the great distance, would you pray to God or row to shore?" Some say one and some say the other, but the right way is to do both. Pray for the strength to row to shore! As the Apostle Paul taught us in Philippians 4:13, "I can do all things through Christ who strengthens me."

Like raising Lazarus from the dead, sometimes God directly fills us with His strength and power to do His work. Other times, He brings brothers and sisters in the Body of Christ to help us, so, like Lazarus, we can be freed to live life to the fullest! Let's confess our areas of sin to Jesus and to safe and significant others because, in doing so, we are promised that we will be healed.

Discussion Questions

1. As we journey through life, we discover areas of our life where we are not free. As we grow in Christ, we can apply God's Word to these areas and see new growth and freedom. What are some of these areas in your life?

_____

_____

_____

_____

_____

2. If you were free in these areas, how would your life be different? What would it look like?

_____

_____

_____

_____

_____

_____

3. Just like Lazarus, we may need help from others to be set free. In what ways do you see yourself needing others in the process of becoming free? Who do you think you can ask for help in these areas? Who can you trust with your sins and who should you avoid confessing to?

_____

_____

_____

_____

_____

_____

4. Do you know of Bible studies or support groups that can help with these areas in your life? What other resources do you think you could employ?

_____

_____

_____

_____

_____

_____

_____

5. The authors hope you will use Growing Stronger Groups to experience that support and guidance. As stated earlier, we also highly recommend Celebrate Recovery groups, which have sprung up all over the United States and some other countries.

_____

_____

_____

_____

_____

6. John 8:31–33 promises, "Then you will know the truth, and the truth will set you free." What are some things you can do to bring truth to these areas of your life?

_____

_____

_____

_____

_____

Growing Stronger Guideline #4
With God's Help, Get Rid of It
Lay aside the things that are holding you back.

Chapter Four

THROW OFF EVERYTHING THAT HINDERS!

"Therefore, since we are surrounded by such a great cloud of witnesses,
let us throw off everything that hinders and the sin that so easily
entangles, and let us run with perseverance the race marked out for us."
(Hebrews 12:1)

As you examine your life, especially in light of recent crises, what are some hindrances that are dragging you down? You might be surprised at the list of obstacles you discover.

Take a Closer Look

It could be a negative, legalistic church that is disheartening you. It might be specific people or groups of people who are unfaithful and disloyal to you, sabotaging with constant criticism and deterring with discouragement. It might be bad habits like substance abuse, overeating, rescuing too many people who don't really need it (codependency), excessive shopping, overworking, or a host of other interferences.

Often we are unaware of hidden hindrances, like basing our self-worth on the way a critical parent raised us. Some may have desired and never experienced love from an abusive father. As a result, they may be addicted to jerks, jumping from the one harmful relationship to another, unconsciously and erroneously trying to fix what went wrong in childhood. Adult children of alcoholics, for example, often marry alcoholics in a vain attempt to fix their family of origin issues.

Dr. Meier once treated a famous movie star who was depressed because she was going through her sixth divorce. All six of her husbands seemed to be really nice when she dated them, but once she got married, each one turned out to be either a drug addict or an alcoholic. All six openly ran around on her and beat her up if she complained about it, and she thought this was all just bad luck!

The movie star grew up with an alcoholic father who had multiple affairs, regularly beat up her mother, and repeatedly sexually abused her as a child. Her mother knew about the sexual abuse and did not protect her. As an adult, it was almost as if she had unconscious antennas attracting her to guys who pretended to be nice but, in reality, behaved horribly, just like her father.

By marrying these men, she was trying to fix her father, win the father-type love she had been missing, get vengeance on her father, and act out a host of other unconscious motives. She had no idea that this extreme area of codependency was ruling and ruining her life, bringing her to crisis after crisis, and breaking her heart. She was most hindered by repressed emotions, motives, and drives deep in her soul about which she was completely unaware. In her case, only professional counseling would bring her to these insights and deliver her from herself.

If you were blessed with loving parents and are free from significant, unconscious hindrances, then thank God for your good fortune. You may have even enjoyed a wonderful childhood with parents who loved you dearly and cheered you on to many successes in your life. Even so, if you want to run strong and last long in this race called the Christian life, you must free yourself from things that hold you back. As loved ones who have gone before are cheering us on, those who follow now are witnessing our race. Because children usually do what we do, not just what we say, they are eagerly watching us, searching for inspiration they so desperately need to keep running!

What's Holding You Back?

The first step toward freedom involves a decision on our part. We must ask, "Am I willing to let go of those things which have hindered me?" Until we respond with a resounding, "Yes!" we remain encumbered. These burdens don't just fall off. We must actively cast away anything that impedes our effectiveness. Then others can follow our example and throw off the weights that hold them back.

Bondage can come in many forms. James 3:2 says we all fail in many ways. Perfection is in the next life, not this one! None of us is exempt as 1 John 1:8 states, "If we claim to be without sin, we deceive ourselves and the truth is not in us." Even the very godly Apostle Paul confessed to the whole world in Romans 6 and 7 that he sometimes did things he should not have done.

But Paul concludes these confessions in Romans 8:1 with the glorious words, "There is therefore now NO CONDEMNATION…" God does not condemn us for our sins. He loves us and wants us to learn and grow from them. King Solomon taught us in the Proverbs that even if a person falls seven times, a righteous person will continue to get up again and again. God helps us to rise to our feet again, as He is a God of grace and growth.

As Christian therapists, it is so sad to see a client, severely abused as a child, who continues to develop damaging relationships because she is familiar with that abusive pattern. It is not uncommon to see a client make great progress, perhaps breaking up with a boyfriend who is beating and raping her, only to watch her run back to him. This is not an inevitable response, however, because with God's help, anyone who really wants healing can get it, no matter how difficult the situation may be.

We have also witnessed the great successes of women who have suffered abuse, yet refused to accept a victim mentality. These courageous women grew from victim to survivor and finally, with God's help, to overcomer as they began to flourish once again. This passage from victim to overcomer requires, first of all, a conscious decision to rise from devastation, then action steps which propel her toward a new destiny.

Do You Want to Be Free?

In John 5:1–15 (NKJV), we find the story of a man at the Pool of Bethesda. He suffered from a physical condition which had disabled him for thirty-eight years. He was lying by the pool with a great number of people with various disabilities, waiting for a certain time when an angel went down into the pool and stirred the water. Whoever managed to step into the water first was healed of their disease.

Jesus came to the pool and saw this man lying there. Knowing that he had endured the infirmity a long time, Jesus asked him, "Do you want to be made well?" (v. 6).

Do you want to be made well? What a strange question to ask a man who had been waiting so long to be healed!

The sick man replied, "Sir, I have no man to put me into the pool when the water is stirred up; but while I am coming, another steps down before me" (v. 7).

He did not realize that he was, at that very moment, speaking with the Son of God who had created him and all the angels! Jesus did not reveal Himself or scold this man for his helpless and hopeless attitude. He simply said, "Rise, take up your bed and walk."

Immediately—after thirty-eight long years—the man was healed, picked up his bed, and walked! He still didn't even know who had healed him, because Jesus quietly slipped away into the crowd.

Only later did Jesus come and find him in the temple, worshipping with the rest of his community. Once again, Jesus said the unexpected, "See, you have been made well. Sin no more, lest a worse thing come upon you" (v.15). Apparently, this man's continued health depended on his choices! The majority of our illnesses are NOT the result of sin in our lives. They may be due to genetic factors, poor nutrition, or a host of other reasons. Generally speaking, we suffer illnesses and tragedies because we live in a fallen world. But in this case, the man bore some responsibility if he wanted to stay well.

Now Jesus is challenging us through His Word, to throw off everything that hinders! Like the man at the pool, we can choose how we will respond to Him. Initially, the man was focused on the angel stirring the water. It was the only hope he had, until that very moment. He had no support system and had wearied of trying on his own.

When the Son of God spoke to him, he couldn't see past his own "stuckness" to the miraculous possibilities right in front of him! He responded with excuses—it's always been this way. Jesus gave him an assignment which required not only faith, but obedient action. He believed, obeyed, and was healed!

Similarly, it's very possible for the things that bog us down and ensnare our steps to masquerade as old friends. We may not be fully aware of our need for change. Or perhaps we do recognize a need for change, but our misguided coping patterns have morphed into destructive habits. We want to be free, but can too easily become accustomed to the familiarity of our fetters. To venture out into freedom requires change, which can appear frightening. Or we try to change, fail, and, like the man at the pool, remain defeated, hopeless, and helpless.

Considering all these challenges, how do we deal with the tendency to hang on to old baggage? We must actively resist the tendency toward complacency. If we want to be free, our first and most important decision requires both faith and action: THROW IT OFF!

With God's Help, Get Rid of It!

When we are finally ready to make that decision, what comes next? White-knuckling it may work for a while, but deep and permanent change requires more than a decision plus will power. To change directions in life, we need clear guidance and lots of support.

Recovery programs such as Alcoholics Anonymous or Celebrate Recovery (a biblically-based Twelve Steps model) encourage participants to begin by admitting their powerlessness over destructive addictions and harmful habits.

This is nothing new. Even the Apostle Paul wrote, "I know that nothing good lives in me, that is, in my sinful nature. For I have the desire to do what is good, but I cannot carry it out" (Romans 7:18). Sound familiar?

Paul knew, all too well, his inability to follow through with his desire to live up to God's standards. He had to come to the end of himself and look to God. For one to arrive at this realization requires true humility, which often accompanies a sense of brokenness. This kind of brokenness is a good thing! While it can be painful, it is the doorway to deliverance!

God promises in Psalm 51:17 that He will not despise anyone who comes to Him with a broken and contrite heart. And in Isaiah 66:1–2 we read:

> This is what the LORD says: 'Heaven is My throne, and the earth is My footstool. Where is the house you will build for Me? Where will My resting place be? Has not My hand made all these things, and so they came into being?' declares the LORD. 'These are the ones I look on with favor: those who are humble and contrite in spirit, and who tremble at My Word.'

God made it all! He doesn't need anything from us, but the God of the Universe will stop in a heartbeat to take notice of the humble hearer of His Word! Perhaps it's because when we humble ourselves, we resemble His Son, Jesus, who, though He was by very nature, God, took on the form of a man. He denied self-indulgence and submitted to His Father's plan. As a result, God raised Him above every name in Heaven and on earth! (Philippians 2:5–11).

But humility is only the first step. God doesn't stop there! He has good plans in store for those who turn to Him! If we give our lives over to God, rather than a vague Higher Power, it is He Himself who works in us "to will and to act according to His good purpose" (Philippians 2:13). As in the case of the man at the pool, Jesus empowers us to do what we previously could not do in our own strength. Not only does Jesus help us, but He gives us a ready-made support system in the Body of Christ, the Church.

Stay Securely Connected.

In order to benefit from this support system, it is imperative to stay connected to God and other Christians. Isolation can be risky! Be sure to surround yourself with those who understand the importance of discarding destructive behaviors and living a life dedicated to God.

When Mary Beth met her now-husband, Bob, he was a new Christian, a freshman in Bible College, and had just marked a year of sobriety from drugs and alcohol. He told her of his early struggle to stay free from drug usage. One drug supplier would pop over unannounced to Bob's house, bringing his wares. Bob's resolve was greatly tested when the drugs were right in front of him, so he appealed to the Lord to keep this drug dealer away from him.

Several months later, when Bob reported to work at his job in the county courthouse, the police elevator opened to reveal this very same drug dealer. There he was, looking dejected, and handcuffed between two police officers who caught him after a high-speed chase! He was sentenced to the federal penitentiary.

As in Bob's case, it is important to recognize the dangers of denial and avoid the company of compromisers. Why hang around those who are still playing with fire and hope that you won't be burned? To do so would only be fooling yourself. 1 Corinthians 15:33 warns, "Do not be deceived. 'Evil company corrupts good habits'" (NKJV).

Remember that one definition of insanity is doing the same things over and over again but expecting different results. So throw off the hindrance of continuing to hang around with the wrong people. Rather than trying to fit in with this crowd, look for the kind of friends who will "spur one another on to love and good deeds" (Hebrews 10:24).

Stay in the Word.

We must crave God's Word more than our daily food! We are saved by God's grace, but we are transformed as our minds are renewed, daily, by retraining ourselves to think like God thinks. Why continue in the futility of our thinking when God says we can have the very mind of Christ? (1 Corinthians 2:16). God wants you to "Let the Word of Christ dwell in you richly" (Colossians 3:16).

More than recovery, God has GREAT dreams and plans for each of us in partnership with Him! Ephesians 2:10 says, "We are God's handiwork, created in Christ Jesus to do good works, which God prepared in advance for us to do." He wants us to soak up His Word, saturate ourselves in His aspirations, and then ask Him for big things! When we do this, we can be confident that His power will enable us because He has promised, "If you remain in Me and my words remain in you, ask whatever you wish, and it will be done for you" (John 15:7).

Stay the Course.

Not everyone will be thrilled when you decide to throw off what hinders you. Some self-righteous individuals will try to lay false "guilt trips" on you. Even some loving friends who mean well may erroneously accuse you for forsaking some of your hindrances, especially if it means leaving an unhealthy church or relationship.

Others may feel guilty when they see your success because they know that they also need to change. If they are not ready to change, they may attempt to pull you down to their level to silence their guilty conscience. At times like this, remember to keep focused on Jesus, "the author and the finisher of your faith" (Hebrews 12:2, NKJV). He began the good work in you and He completes what He starts! He will continue working in and through you until the day you cross the ultimate finish line in Heaven (Philippians 1:6).

Get Up, Again!

Sometimes people are afraid to start a journey for fear that they will fail. Taking that first step may require putting the fear of failure to rest by realizing that it is actually true: humans will fail. That's why we need a Savior! Jesus is the only perfect human who ever walked this earth. But because He is also fully God, He is able to provide forgiveness and restore us when we are less than perfect!

Remaining aware of our vulnerability will help us to avoid a fall. It's when we are not paying attention that we are the most susceptible to slipping. Paul cautions us, "So, if you think you are standing firm, be careful that you don't fall!" (1 Corinthians 10:12).

If we do fall, however, it is important to remind ourselves to get up again! When we fall, we rise again, not by hiding in shame, but by approaching God's throne of grace with confidence, so that we may receive mercy and find grace to help us in our time of need (Hebrews 4:16)!

This journey of change begins with and is sustained by humility. We confess our sins to God. He forgives and restores us. Then, we confess our sins to and pray for each other. That's how we are healed (James 5:16)! But it isn't safe to confess to just anybody! We must find someone who shares the same humble attitude.

Knowing that we are all vulnerable to the same temptations, Paul instructs us in Galatians 6:1, "Brothers, if someone is caught in a sin, you who are spiritual should restore him gently. But watch yourself, or you also may be tempted." Thankfully, we have a Savior who became man, was tempted in every way we are, overcame the temptations, and now continually prays for us and helps us on our journey.

Discussion Questions

1. How would you describe the "race" you are running? Is it a "marathon" or a "sprint"? Why?

_____

_____

_____

_____

_____

2. When we are young, we think our "race" will last forever. As we get older, we are closer to seeing the "finish line." How does the stage of life you are in right now affect how you are running?

_____

_____

_____

_____

3. Ask God to show you how He sees your "race." Is there anything that is slowing you down from running the way you would like? What would be involved in "throwing off" that hindrance in your life?

_____

_____

_____

_____

4. Remember that we do not run alone or in our own strength. Commit your "race" to God and ask Him to free you from anything that is slowing you down or causing you to stumble.

_____

_____

_____

_____

_____

Keep Looking Up

Make PERSONAL GROWTH an even higher
priority than resolving your current crisis.

Chapter Five

FIX OUR EYES ON JESUS

"Let us fix our eyes on Jesus, the author and perfecter of our faith,
who for the joy set before Him endured the cross, scorning its
shame, and sat down at the right hand of the throne of God."
(Hebrews 12:2)

A True Story

On November 15, 1989, I (Dr. Meier) was driving my car home from work while listening, as I usually did, to the Bible on a cassette tape. I just "happened" to hear Psalm 66 and vaguely remember words like, "men flying over my head but God delivering me from the fire and from the water." What a strange passage, I thought to myself, as I made a left turn at a major intersection.

I was so distracted that I drove straight into an oncoming car, both of us going about forty miles an hour. My car flew high into the air and turned around, front to back, flipping and landing with my roof directly on the pavement. The people driving by seemed to be flying over my head. My car was completely squashed except the driver's seat, where I hung upside down from the seat belt that saved my life. Both cars were totaled, and my front end was destroyed, but God delivered me from the fire and water spewing from my car.

I broke the front window with my elbow and loosened the seat belt so I could crawl out before the car caught fire. As I was flying through the air, before landing upside down, I felt total peace, thinking, "Oh, this is what God has in store for me today." But after I escaped from my car, even though the other driver and I were both unscratched, I was suddenly filled with delayed fear.

Still, I foolishly risked climbing back into my upside-down car to retrieve the cassette tape and my Dallas Cowboy Weekly, which I read religiously! A family who witnessed the accident called 911 and the ambulance was first to respond to the scene. The medic concluded that neither driver had a scratch, so he drove off just as the policeman arrived. The officer observed me next to my car dressed in a suit, and assumed I was a bystander. Supposing that the driver of my car must have died, he asked me if the ambulance driver had just left with the body.

"I am the body," I assured him.

He was astonished that I was unharmed!

That night I had one of my many "God dreams"—dreams in which Jesus appears and tells me specific things that come true the next day. In the dream, Jesus told me to wake up, get the cassette tape, and listen to it in my Walkman until I heard a verse that "knocked me between the eyes." I started listening where I had left off, with Psalm 66, and continued on and on. By then it was 3 a.m., so I asked Jesus to please hurry and give me the right verse, but it took a while. Finally, Jesus "knocked me between the eyes" with Psalm 90:12: "Teach us to number our days, that we may gain a heart of wisdom." From that verse, God showed me that while, statistically speaking, I should not have survived the accident, He wanted me to pretend that I actually had died. As a result, I now wake up each morning realizing that this new day is a gift from God—a bonus day that I do not deserve.

The morning after the accident, I called my mother-in-law to tell her about it. She was only slightly surprised that I had an accident. She informed me that she had been praying, every day for one week, that her sons and daughters and their mates would not die in a car accident.

I could hardly believe it, but since I knew her to be an honest and godly woman, I asked why she would pray such an unusual prayer. She shocked me again by saying that the week before she had gone to bed meditating on Psalm 90:12, "Teach us to number our days…" She had a conviction that one of her children was going to be involved in a serious car accident. She didn't tell any of us about it, but prayed for us individually, by name, every day since that verse impressed her. This was my sign from God that this had, indeed, been a "God dream."

On another occasion, I dreamed that my own daughter stopped suddenly on a highway and was rear-ended by another car. My wife and I prayed for her safety that day. That very afternoon, she called from California to inform us that she was driving down a highway at seventy mph when her brakes suddenly locked! The car behind her crashed into her, but no one was hurt!

Is it possible that many so-called "coincidences" are actually God secretly intervening in our lives in ways that we do not recognize? Keeping our eyes fixed on Jesus will help us realize that His hand is at work in our daily circumstances. As we are aware of God's presence, we are reminded of Psalm 139:5: "You have enclosed me behind and before, and laid Your hand upon me" (NASB). In other words, He is hugging us with one arm and leading us with the other!

As a result of my car accident on November 15, 1989, and the dreams, events, and meditations that followed, I developed a four-point prayer which I have prayed almost every morning since. You will find all four of these principles incorporated into our Twelve Growing Stronger Guidelines for overcoming and growing from crises.

Dr. Meier's Four-Point Morning Prayer:

1. **"Lord, help me to become more like You today."** Because of this simple prayer, I am able to fix my eyes on Jesus. If anything goes wrong that day, I can thank God, even in the middle of the problem, because I know it will help me accomplish the desire I prayed for that very morning—to become more like Jesus. Without hardships and disappointments I will not grow very rapidly. I also pray that God will help me be a good listener and learn as much as possible the easy way!

2. **"Lord, help me to serve You today."** My goal is not for personal gain, but for God to reach out, in love, through me that day to "dance with the world" in some way that will bless at least one person.

3. **"Lord, help me to stay out of trouble today."** I know I am a sinner, fully capable of sins of omission or commission. But all sin hurts somebody—God, others, or me—so I really do not want to yield to the temptation to sin.

4. **"Lord, help me to learn and grow from whatever may go wrong today."** I expect to lead a normal life, and all normal lives include some setbacks, failures, and crises. I expect to suffer one or more disappointments each day. When most days go by without one, I consider those bonus days!

I have a totally different perspective than I had before the accident. I am able to fix my eyes on Jesus and see things from an eternal perspective. I used to get angry, even with God, when I experienced disappointments and crises. I would be surprised and even shocked by them, as though, somehow, I was entitled to a calamity-free life. I also tended to "catastrophize"—to assume the worst scenario—when trouble did arise. Now I can step back a bit, gain perspective, and realize that God will help me through whatever comes my way. In fact, He will even use it to grow me up!

Focus, Focus...

This new kind of perspective emerges from repeatedly choosing to focus our eyes on Jesus. What a beautiful alternative to constantly paying attention to ourselves and our problems! It is only natural for humans to be somewhat self-absorbed. It is easy to turn our gaze inward and concentrate on our own needs and wants. But as we see our trials through God's eyes, we increase our capacity to give of ourselves to others. Our generous example, then, will encourage others to do the same.

When the Bible uses the term "fix," it is not referring to a casual glance, but purposefully turning away from one thing to focus on something else. It is difficult to fix our eyes on our problems and on Jesus at the same time. But deliberately pondering His insight on our predicaments is very practical, since obsessing about our struggles doesn't work anyway! That only causes anxiety, grief, and stress. Jesus has better solutions to our problems.

A Far-sighted Perspective

Sometimes ordeals loom so large that it is hard to think about anything else. That's when faith and patience help us turn our gaze away from the circumstances and toward Jesus, who can give us an entirely new view. When Dr. Meier taught at Dallas Theological Seminary for twelve years, he had a student who is now a good friend, Pastor Tony Evans. In a sermon, Pastor Tony taught that standing right next to a tall, downtown skyscraper could cause one to feel very small. Yet, spotting that same building from an airplane provides a completely different perception. Maintaining this farsighted outlook can remind us that God has the power to work everything out for us, according to His higher purposes.

A building at the center of Biola University, in La Mirada, California, displays a beautiful, thirty-foot-tall mural of Jesus. He is dressed in a red robe and holding out a large black Bible. Often referred to as "The Jesus Mural," this stunning work, gifted to the campus by talented muralist Kent Twitchell in 1990, is officially entitled, "The Word." The artwork incorporates a large, live olive tree. This tree symbolizes the Jews (God's chosen people) and anyone who, by believing in Jesus, is "grafted" into that olive tree as part of God's special family. In addition to its beauty, those who walk by are often amazed that, because of the mural's height, it appears that Jesus' gaze is always upon them (Mural Conservancy of Los Angeles n.d.).

We know, from Psalm 139, that God has been closely watching over us, keenly interested in every aspect of our lives, from our very conception until this moment. Now, He is asking that we keep our eyes on Him! As we do, we will soon realize that no matter how big our problems may appear, Jesus is much, much BIGGER!

From Crisis to Opportunity

While we can take comfort in Romans 8:28 (that God will work everything together for our good), Romans 8:29 is every bit as important as verse 28. In verse 29 we learn that Jesus "foreknew" that you would become a believer someday. Other passages in the Bible inform us that before God even created this world, He could look into the future and know you personally and intimately. Verse 29 continues that God's goal for your life is for you to become conformed to the image of Christ. This means that God wants you to develop deeper and deeper character and love, like the character and love of Jesus.

Think about that for a minute or two. When you have a crisis, God loves you and feels empathy for you. Jesus knows how you feel because He also suffered many trials during His earthly life. He wants to help you. But from His eternal perspective, resolving this situation is just a very small part of the picture. His larger goal is to conform you to the image of Christ. Hopefully, you will experience a good, long life here on earth. But you will enjoy a perfect life, forever with Him in Heaven. He wants to help you solve your problems, but He will use what you learn from this temporary crisis as a tool in His hands to carve you into a beautiful woman of character.

But maximizing trials to conform you to the image of Jesus does not mean that God brought this trouble upon you. We live in a fallen world where we will have tribulation as Jesus said in John 16:33. But He offers us His peace because He has overcome the world! The Bible also says that God is never the author of sin. He never, ever causes anyone to sin against you. He is angry when anyone abuses you in any way. But after He helps you overcome this present difficulty, He promises to make you stronger than ever!

The Bible says we can be thankful in all things, but it takes a real saint to be thankful in the moment a crisis arrives. Sometimes we succeed, but often it is difficult. One Christmas morning, I (Dr. Meier) had to make quick and quite early hospital rounds, visiting my patients before going home to open presents with my children. On my way home, I ran over a nail and got a really bad flat tire. To top it all off, my spare tire was flat, too! I would need outside help on Christmas day.

Fortunately, that morning I had been meditating on being thankful in every situation. I briefly paused to pray, "Thank you, Lord, for allowing me to have this flat tire. Help my children and me to grow from this experience and not to be bitter about it."

When I looked up from prayer, I saw an open gas station down the road to my right. I slowly drove on my flat tire the few hundred feet to the station where the attendant sold me just the tire I needed! He also fixed the one with a nail to use as my spare. In addition, when he learned that I was a psychiatrist, he related his personal story of a crisis with me. I was able to share Jesus with him and he accepted Jesus into his life! The whole process took less than thirty minutes!

Needless to say, I drove home celebrating the fact that I had a flat tire that day! I was able to share this experience with my children before we had our usual Christmas devotions and then opened our presents.

Freedom from Focusing on Our Fear

Fixing our eyes on Jesus can protect us from fears of loss and failure. Although we all suffer loss, we do not have to fear that it will destroy us. In fact, when we live for Jesus, even bad news eventually becomes good news as He turns it around for our benefit.

The Bible tells of great men such as Joseph, Moses, David, and Daniel who endured immeasurable injury and sorrow. In all these cases, as they remained faithful to God, their distress eventually resulted in victory as God caused them to rise above it and even bless those who persecuted them.

Sometimes we are tempted to focus on our fears. When we feel fearful, it is good to remember that nine out of ten things we fear will never happen, and we grow from the ones that do! When we ask our older clients what caused their greatest growth spurt emotionally and spiritually, they nearly always list their greatest loss or failure. Of course, we don't recommend looking for failure, but we all fail in many ways. Others fail us, too. So when failure does occur, learn and grow from it while better understanding how to protect yourself and your loved ones in the future.

Abraham Lincoln went bankrupt twice and lost some loved ones to death. All of this strengthened and prepared him to become one of the greatest Presidents this world has ever seen. It was Abraham Lincoln who, later in life, observed, "Most folks are about as happy as they make up their minds to be" (Quotes.net, STANDS4 LLC, 2014. "Abraham Lincoln Quotes." n.d.). This very quote inspired Dr. Meier to name his second book, *Happiness is a Choice*. It was published in 1977, sold over a million copies, and was revised and rereleased in 2013. Choosing happiness doesn't mean you can turn it on like a light switch. But it does mean you can choose to focus on Jesus, deliberately take steps to recover (such as the Twelve Growing Stronger Guidelines in this book), and eventually find happiness at the other end of the tunnel.

Avoid Destructive Distractions

God knows that we get into trouble if we don't look to Jesus. If we seek anything other than Jesus to fill the hole in our soul, we become vulnerable to addictions. Substitutes, such as food, TV, computers, chat rooms, video games, sex, pornography, romance novels, sports, gambling, excess shopping, alcohol, drugs, and even people, only serve to increase our longings. Only God can quench the thirst of our hearts. He is eternally satisfying. He's a perfect fit. Everything else leaks! Of course, He wants us to find intimacy with one or more people as well, but human relationships will not fill the place in our hearts that only God can satisfy.

Distracted by "The Good"

Sometimes we simply get distracted from the Lord and fix our eyes on other things. Even good things, if deterring us from God's ways, become hindrances.

Luke 10:38–42 tells about two sisters who had the wonderful opportunity of hosting Jesus in their home. What an honor! As the story unfolded, though, we see that the sisters responded to the situation in two very different ways. While Martha extended the invitation and began all the preparations to serve Jesus, her sister Mary sat at Jesus' feet and heard His teaching.

Martha was a conscientious hostess, but got a little carried away. She was so worried and anxious about working for Jesus that she forgot to take the time to enjoy Him as Mary did. When Martha complained to Jesus about Mary not helping her, instead of scolding Mary and sending her into the kitchen, Jesus tenderly called Martha by name, twice! He acknowledged that she was distracted about many things and taught her the one essential that brings everything else into focus: turning her attention to Jesus. He surprised Martha by encouraging her to become more like Mary.

"Only one thing is needed", Jesus said. "Mary has chosen what is better, and it will not be taken away from her" (vs. 42).

I (Mary Beth) have often contemplated the irony of my own name, as I have a strong tendency to be a "Martha" rather than a "Mary." I have been blessed with good endurance and a strong work ethic, but I regularly have to rein myself in from overworking. Like Mary, I absolutely LOVE to spend time "sitting at Jesus' feet," reading the Bible and praying. One of the greatest joys in my life has been meeting with dear friends for Bible study and prayer. Still, I have to be careful not to be bullied by the busyness of my to-do lists, or I am in danger of going into full-blown "Martha-mode." My family would tell you that we have much more peace and joy in our home if my heart maintains a "Mary posture," at the feet of Jesus, as I go about my daily work.

Stay Alert.

Finally, in our efforts to focus on Jesus, we must remain aware of the fact that we have an enemy who would love to derail us. He is more than happy to throw temptation before us in the form of the cares of this world, the deceitfulness of riches, and the desire for other things (Mark 4:19).

Another role of the devil is to accuse Christians. He will try to discourage you, shake your confidence, and even try to make you hate yourself. He amplifies the negative self-talk which you may have learned from hurtful people in your childhood. He tries to convince you to give up in times of crisis. He will attempt to distract or discourage you. But either way, his ultimate goal is to destroy you. That's why 1 Peter 5:8 cautions us to "Be self-controlled and alert. Your enemy the devil prowls around like a roaring lion looking for someone to devour."

Aside from outward influences, our own weak flesh can also lead us off track. Even the necessary routines of daily life and the resulting fatigue can cause us to faint and lose focus. Fortunately, in Christ we have the protection we need to defeat the enemy and the power of the Holy Spirit to overcome the weaknesses of our flesh.

A United Focus

We can also take courage as we continually remind ourselves that we do not have to do this alone. The Scripture says, "Let US fix OUR eyes." (Hebrews 12:2, emphasis ours). As the Body of Christ, we are in this together as we look to Jesus: our example, our helper, our teacher, our source, our comforter, our "Older Brother," our God, the author and perfecter of our faith!

Discussion Questions

1. The Lord's Prayer begins with "Our Father, who art in Heaven, hallowed be Thy name" (Matthew 6:9). Jesus was teaching us to get our eyes on God and His character before we tell Him about our prayer needs. Take a few moments and list some of the ways we can "hallow His name"—bring praise and glory to His name.

_____

_____

_____

_____

_____

2. Read the account of Peter walking on the water in Matthew 14:22–33. What caused Peter to walk on the water? What caused Peter to be afraid? What happened when he was afraid? How does this apply to your most recent crisis?

_____

_____

_____

_____

3. In the story above, what was Jesus' assessment of the problem that caused Peter to begin to sink.

_____

_____

_____

_____

4. Taking our eyes off Jesus and looking at the storm around us can cause us to falter in our faith. Focusing on Jesus strengthens our faith, as He is the author and perfecter of our faith! Consider what situations in your life have caused you to look at "the wind" instead of Jesus. Take a moment now to praise the Lord for His wonderful name, and then release those cares to Him.

_____

_____

_____

_____

_____

5. Share with whomever you are with right now at least one crisis that you remember. In what ways have you grown stronger than you ever were before as a result of working through that crisis?

_____

_____

_____

_____

_____

Chapter Six

FOR THE JOY SET BEFORE YOU ... ENDURE!

"Let us fix our eyes on Jesus, the author and perfector of our faith, who for the joy set before Him endured the cross, scorning its shame, and sat down at the right hand of the throne of God."
(Hebrews 12:2)

Hang in There!

Endurance!! The challenges of life can be really tough sometimes! Even Thomas Edison, an absolute genius and one of the greatest inventors of all time, declared, "Genius is one percent inspiration, and ninety-nine percent perspiration" (Quotes.net, STANDS4 LLC, 2014. "Thomas Edison Quotes." n.d.). Although it was hard work, because Edison persevered through many failed inventions, we can now easily flip a switch and enjoy incandescent light—just one of his many inventions of great value. His dreams spurred him on to overcome obstacles.

Helen Keller is another courageous example of endurance. As a toddler, Helen's sight and hearing were destroyed by a mysterious and extremely high fever. She triumphed over deafness and blindness to become an author, speaker, and world-renowned humanitarian. Recognized by Winston Churchill as "the greatest woman of our age" (Helen Keller Foundation n.d.), Helen was the first deaf and blind person to receive a Bachelor of Arts degree. She also received honorary doctorate degrees from six universities around the world, including Harvard, and met every American President from Grover Cleveland to Lyndon B. Johnson (Keller).

An inspiration to those of us who struggle with far less, Helen exhorted, "We differ, blind and seeing, one from another, not in our senses, but in the use we make of them, in the imagination and courage with which we seek wisdom beyond the senses." And again, "A happy life consists not in the absence, but in the mastery of hardships" (Helen Keller Biography n.d.).

But behind this great woman was another great woman, Helen's teacher, Anne Sullivan, who also had overcome great adversity. Born into extreme poverty, Anne suffered the loss of many family members by death or desertion. At age five, her eyesight was severely damaged by a disease called Trachoma. Anne and her little brother Jimmy were sent to live at the poor house, where Jimmy died three months later (Anne Sullivan Biography n.d.).

Alone and desperate for a better life, Anne escaped the poor house by going to Perkins School for the Blind. Not only did Anne learn braille and receive an education, but she later underwent surgery which restored much of her eyesight. Although Anne was quite ignorant, academically and socially when she began her schooling, she graduated as valedictorian of her class! In June 1886, she delivered a graduation speech where she challenged her fellow students, "Duty bids us go forth into active life. Let us go cheerfully, hopefully, and earnestly, and set ourselves to find our special part. When we have found it, willingly and faithfully perform it; for every obstacle we overcome, every success we achieve tends to bring man closer to God" (Sullivan).

With this clear mission, Anne went on to become Helen Keller's teacher. She used the braille skills she had learned at Perkins to unlock the turbulent, dark, and silent world in which Helen lived. Because Anne had also been a troubled and difficult child afflicted with blindness, she was able to love Helen despite Helen's early tantrums and obstinacy. She didn't give up, and through faith, love, and perseverance, she found the jewel of a girl trapped inside Helen's little deaf and blind body. Without the challenges that Anne had overcome and her resulting sense of mission, she never would have reached Helen and equipped her to become one of the most inspirational women of all time.

First Anne needed to teach Helen the very concept of language, and then she led her to explore the wonderful new life before her. Later, Helen described when she learned her first word, water: "The mystery of language was revealed to me. I knew then that "w-a-t-e-r" meant the wonderful cool something that was flowing over my hand. That living word awakened my soul, gave it light, hope, joy, set it free!" (Helen Keller Biography n.d.). Helen continues to describe the arduous learning process: "Gradually from naming an object we advance step by step until we have traversed the vast distance between our first stammered syllable and the sweep of thought in a line of Shakespeare" (Keller n.d.).

Heroes, such as Edison, Keller, and Sullivan can encourage and inspire us to carry on when life gets tough. But only one "hero," Jesus, will be ever-present when difficulties may tempt us to feel as though we can't go on. At these points, it is critical that we consider His example as the author and perfecter of our faith. As the author of our faith, Christ has given us new life. As the perfecter of our faith, He won't give up on us in hard times but will use those difficult periods to continue to refine us, not define us!

How Did Jesus Do It?

As we "fix our eyes" on Jesus, we see the perfect example of endurance. How did Jesus do it? First of all He endured the cross. Yes, Jesus was fully God, but, amazingly, He was fully human as well. His physical body felt every lash of the whip, every nail, every excruciating breath. More than 700 years before the birth of Jesus, the Prophet Isaiah described Jesus' appearance as so disfigured that it was "beyond that of any man and His form marred beyond human likeness" (Is. 52:14), yet He endured it!

Jesus endured the cross. But why did He do this? And how was it possible? Hebrews 12:2 says that the "joy set before Him" helped Him to endure. Jesus did not suffer for nothing! What was the "joy" that helped Him endure such torment? In short, WE are His joy. WE are His reward for suffering!

When we are suffering, depression can attempt to lead us to the misbelief that there is no way out—no light at the end of the tunnel. But the authors of this book, through our therapy work, rejoice with those who have endured and found the joy at the end of the tunnel of pain. We too must have faith that there is "joy set before us" and endure until we get there. As Mary Beth's husband Bob often says, "One day, this pain will fade and will seem like a distant memory. Then there will be joy again."

Jesus had to be willing to live in a flesh-and-blood body in order to be like us. But because He was also fully God, when He suffered death he accomplished several amazing things. First of all, He tasted death for everyone. He experienced everything that we suffer as humans, even every type of temptation to fail or give up.

Secondly, He paid the price to bring all those who will believe in Him to Heaven. He took the sins of the world upon Himself and died, once for all, so that we could live eternally. He blazed the way for us to become children of God.

Thirdly, He destroyed the devil who holds the power of death. Our enemy's death sentence has already been signed, and will, in God's time, be executed.

Finally, He freed us from the slavery of the fear of death! By rising from the dead, He defeated death itself! As Christians, we know that the end of this life is only the beginning of eternal life with Christ. What an amazing purchase and what an incredible price He paid! Our eternal destinies hung in the balance and were guaranteed life because He endured to the end.

It's Easier to Endure When You Understand "The Why."

What if Jesus had not endured? What if He had not paid the purchase price for us? How many times have we decided to quit when faced with much lesser challenges? Jesus knew exactly why the Father had sent Him into the world. "For God did not send His Son into the world to condemn the world, but that the world through Him might be saved" (John 3:17, NKJV). Thank God Jesus didn't give up halfway to the cross! He is our example to never surrender. Hebrews 12:4 reminds us, "In your struggle against sin, you have not yet resisted to the point of shedding your blood." With His inspiration and His help we can forget what is behind, focus on what is ahead and press on to win the goal and the prize to which God has called us heavenward in Christ Jesus (Philippians 3:13–15).

Jesus Understands When Enduring Gets Hard.

Jesus understands that we will suffer. He knows that life in this fallen world includes seasons of suffering. Yet, He encourages us to "Be of good cheer," because He has overcome the world (John 16:33)!

But how can we "be of good cheer" when we feel defeated and depressed? When things seem hopeless? When we are depressed, a chemical called "serotonin" gets depleted in the brain, influencing us to think that we will never get better. But everyone can overcome depression with the right kind of guidance and assistance. Sometimes this even includes medication for those who inherit a serotonin deficiency (just as God allows some to inherit insufficient thyroid hormones or insulin or any other chemical problem in our bodies).

There is No Shame!

Many of us grew up in homes where we were manipulated through guilt. Rather than receiving mature guidance and correction and even discipline, we were shamed, criticized, and even ridiculed, and we believed the lies of the authority figures in our lives. Others of us grew up in healthy homes but suffered toxic shame from significant other people as we grew older.

When we sin, some guilt is good. This godly sorrow guides us to repent and turn over a new leaf, becoming a better AND FORGIVEN person (2 Corinthians 7:10–11). But shame is false guilt—feeling guilty for things that either are not wrong or have already been forgiven. Sometimes we can even feel false guilt due to wrongs committed against us. If we allow it, shame can defeat us. Our enemy, the devil, and his demons constantly attempt to accuse us. He can even pretend to be an angel of light (2 Corinthians 11:14) and try to make us feel so falsely guilty that we give up, believing that somehow we have failed God. But in reality, God is hugging us with one arm while guiding us to the light with His other outstretched arm.

We can also fear feeling ashamed before our peers. A failed marriage, a rebellious child, a temporary relapse into a personal addiction, financial loss, bankruptcy, and many other crises can be embarrassing to us. We want others to see us in a good light, forgetting that it is normal for all human beings to experience various failures throughout life. In reality, our clients are often shocked to find that admitting their failures to significant others results in those people loving them even more—not less.

Beyond endurance, the Bible also tells us that Jesus "scorned the shame" of the cross (Hebrews 12:2). Not only did He suffer the unbelievable physical pain of the crucifixion, but He understands feelings of isolation, rejection, and shame. The Prophet Isaiah described, "He was despised and rejected by men, a man of sorrows and familiar with suffering. Like one from whom men hide their faces he was despised, and we esteemed him not" (Isaiah 53:3).

Jesus faced a mock trial, was publicly humiliated, betrayed, falsely accused, abandoned by friends, slandered, and taunted, but His response to all this was to scorn the shame. Jesus shamed the shame! He didn't despise the people who were rejecting Him and subjecting Him to humiliation, but He did recognize the shame for what it was and did not allow it to work its way inside His heart or color His perception of Himself! Jesus knew who He was. He did not allow Himself to be defined by what others did to Him or said about Him.

Jesus had no reason to feel ashamed. He had never done anything wrong. In contrast, every one of us has sinned, resulting in true guilt until we confess it. The good news is that because Jesus took the shame of our sin upon Himself on the cross, we can now live free from shame!

In fact, Psalm 34:5 promises, "Those who look to Him are radiant; their faces are never covered with shame."

There are Rewards Ahead!

After Jesus endured the pain and scorned the shame, He received the acclaim of His Father in Heaven. As we endure hardship and scorn the shame, we can expect that God will also bring good out of our situation. As an unknown author has said, "Everything will be okay in the end. If it's not okay, it's not the end!"

When we face adversity, it is natural to wonder whether we are in God's will. We want to know God's will for our lives. Romans 8:39 says that His primary will is for us to become more like Jesus, "conformed to the image of Christ." God still wants us to be our own unique selves but to become better equipped to love and be loved, just like Jesus loves and is loved.

Have you ever had the experience of remarking about how a child resembled her mother, only to find out that she was adopted? Or have you ever noticed a couple who have been married for many years and actually begin to look like each other? Since we have been adopted as God's children, He wants to see the family resemblance in us! In Hebrews 2:11, we read that Jesus is not embarrassed to call us His sisters and brothers. As we spend time with God, we begin to look more and more like His Son Jesus! 2 Corinthians 3:18 says that we will be "transformed into His likeness with ever-increasing glory, which comes from the Lord, who is the Spirit."

Enduring hard times with God's help, rejecting shame, and growing to be more like Jesus leads to the abundant life that He came to bring us. When adversity tries to intimidate us, we can follow Christ's example and endure—and even rejoice—while looking by faith to a better future. We can "consider it all joy" (James 1:2–4), knowing that this testing time will result in greater endurance and maturity. We will grow through our pain and come out whole at the other end. Our faith, though tested by fire, will shine like gold in the end, which will bring glory and honor to God.

So don't grow weary and lose heart. Keep Christ in focus and heavenly rewards in mind. With God's help, if we will:

- endure the pain and
- scorn the shame, we will
- receive the acclaim of our Father in Heaven!

Then He will say, "Well done, good and faithful servant; you were faithful over a few things, I will make you ruler over many things. Enter into the joy of your Lord" (Matthew 25:21).

Discussion Questions

1. The opposite of enduring is quitting! What is at stake if you quit? What do you stand to gain if you endure?

_____

_____

_____

_____

_____

2. We have an enemy whose methods are to steal, kill, and destroy; including his efforts to keep us from fulfilling the destiny (the race marked out for us) that God has in store. The Apostle Paul taught us in 2 Corinthians 2:11 that we must be aware of his schemes so that he might not outwit us. What are some things against which you can be on your guard so that the enemy does not succeed in his efforts to make you give up the race? How can you strengthen yourself in these areas?

_____

_____

_____

_____

_____

3. How did Jesus strengthen Himself in times of trial, enabling Him to endure until he succeeded in His terrible death and glorious resurrection? How can you implement these strategies in your life?

_____

_____

_____

_____

_____

4. The Apostle Peter taught us in 1 Peter 5:8–9 to be self-controlled and alert against the enemy's tactics, resisting him while standing firm in the faith, knowing that other Christians throughout the world are experiencing similar sufferings. Fellowship with other Christians helps us stand strong. With whom can you fellowship to help you stand strong and endure?

_____

_____

_____

_____

_____

Chapter Seven

ACCEPT THE LORD'S DISCIPLINE

"Moreover, we have all had human fathers who disciplined us and we respected them for it. How much more should we submit to the Father of our spirits and live!"
(Hebrews 12:9)

It Hurts So Good!

Discipline: nobody likes it, but everybody needs it. We don't suggest that you pray for it, but when it does come, accept discipline as coming from a loving Father! Pray that God will teach you "the easy way" whenever possible, yet understand that He sometimes uses discipline to get our attention. We can pray that God will lighten our burden, or we can pray that He will strengthen our back. Praying for both is also a good idea!

In the Bible, we read an entire book about the experiences of Job, who was a moral, loving and innocent man, but nevertheless suffered a severe crisis involving a horrible and painful skin disease and eventually the death of his own children. His wife and friends gave him what God Himself called bad advice, telling him it must be due to sins Job had committed. But it wasn't. It was just a crisis God allowed for a variety of reasons none of us will completely understand until we get to Heaven and ask Him. When Job's wife was attempting to lay this false guilt trip upon Job, Job correctly and wisely replied, "What? Shall we expect good from God and not also expect adversity?" (Job 2:10). God wants good things for our lives but sometimes allows us to suffer because of the sins of others or because of circumstances beyond our control. So if you are in a crisis, search to see if it is the discipline of the Lord because of sin in your life, but don't let people lay a guilt trip on you if it isn't.

Testimony from Dr. Meier

In my own case, I would like to confess to you two painful incidents that happened to me as a result of my own sin of pride—one in Russia and one in Cuba, of all places.

My books have been read by millions of people in over twenty languages. I have traveled all over the world training pastors, missionaries, lay counselors, and professionals in Christian, biblically-based psychology. When I start to get proud of myself, without fail I experience God's discipline.

I was in Russia after Yeltsin's soldiers (at least temporarily) ended Communist rule. I was toasting his soldiers with my Coca Cola. I was invited to teach future Russian psychologists for over a week in St. Petersburg. About half of them trusted Christ in the process! I saw miraculous things happen.

The last night there, I was in my hotel room, all alone in the dark, overlooking the Baltic Sea. In my prayers, I started telling the Lord how lucky He was to have me. An hour or so later, I experienced a dream where Jesus told me, "Paul, I choose the foolish things of the world to confound the wise." Then many of the sins I had committed, from early childhood until that date, flashed before my eyes. I woke up weeping and asking God to forgive me for my pride. Then I felt total peace from the Holy Spirit and felt His presence in a unique way. I told nobody about the dream.

At our devotions the next morning, the leader said he had intended to share a different verse, but in a dream the previous night, God led him to share the verse about God choosing the foolish things of the world to confound the wise. I had the chills. It had to be one chance in ten thousand or more that his verse would be the same as mine, and one chance in the millions that we would both dream about it the same night in the same Russian city.

A few years later, I traveled with a team to two cities in Cuba where I taught Christian psychology to about a thousand Cuban physicians. Some of these physicians were even members of Fidel Castro's cabinet. They were all devout atheists whose lives were threatened if they came to believe in God. Castro's spy accompanied me every step of the way to be sure I did not say anything bad about him or his government. Part of our group held children's meetings where they were able to lead hundreds of Cuban children to Christ! The night before our team left, I had completely forgotten what the Lord had taught me in St. Petersburg a few years earlier. I started telling the Lord how lucky He was to have me again. Some people just don't learn well!!

An hour later, I had the same "Jesus dream." This time, He told me that His strength is made perfect in weakness, and my weakness was my greatest qualification for Him to use me, so that He could get the glory, rather than me. I wept, apologized, and then felt total peace. Again, I told nobody the dream.

The next morning, the devotional leader told how, in a dream the night before, God had shown him a verse, which he decided to share instead of the one he had originally planned… You guessed it! "My strength is made perfect in weakness" (2 Corinthians 12:9).

There are 150 verses in the Bible about how God uses dreams and speaks to us in the "night seasons." But one of my favorites is from Job, who suffered greatly—even without any personal sin involved—for God's glory. Job said:

> For God speaks again and again, though people do not recognize it. He speaks in dreams, in visions of the night, when deep sleep falls on people as they lie in their beds. He whispers in their ears and terrifies them with warnings. He makes them turn from doing wrong; he keeps them from pride. He protects them from the grave, from crossing over the river of death. .....listen to me. Keep silent and I will teach you wisdom!" (Job 33:14–18, 33:33, NLT).

God is a Good Father!

We are God's children. Though He must discipline us at times, He is not an abusive father, but a loving heavenly Father, who rebukes, corrects, and, yes, sometimes even punishes His children. We can be sure that God's discipline is helping us to look more like His Son, our Big Brother Jesus.

As good parents, we would not consider neglecting the discipline of our children. Sometimes, especially with a strong-willed child, it can be a very difficult task. We persist, however, for we know that, "The rod of correction imparts wisdom, but a child left to himself disgraces his mother" (Proverbs 29:15). We want our children to obey us for their own good. If we respect our human fathers for disciplining us, "how much more should we submit to the Father of our spirits and live!" (Hebrews 12:9).

Sometimes God corrects us, even in little things, for our own good and to bless others. It may not always make sense to us, but God has His reasons. Recently, I (Mary Beth) had such an opportunity to experience my Father's gentle course correction.

One morning, I had so much to do that I prayed for peace and asked God, "Please, order my steps." I knew my tendency to worry, like Martha, about so many things to do, but in my heart, I wanted to be like Mary and at least "sit at Jesus' feet" as I went about my work. With my to-do list before me, I repeated Proverbs 16:3 to the Lord as I prayed about the day ahead, "Commit your actions to the LORD, and your plans will succeed" (NLT). "Thank you, Lord, that You care about what concerns me today," I prayed.

I also knew that sometimes I could run ahead of God with my own plans, so I prayed, "Help me, Lord, not to be rebellious if You direct me a way that I don't really want to go. I know that Your ways are best. Please, go before me and even help me to obey You."

I needed to stop at a department store and also pick up a few things at the hardware store. I headed to the hardware store but felt a nudge in my heart to go to the department store first.

"Hmm, that's funny," I thought. "I wonder why the Lord would care which store I go to first…" But since I had prayed, I followed that "still, small voice" and headed to the department store.

I collected the items on my list and then felt an urgency to pay and get going. Again, I thought that was curious, but I have walked with the Lord long enough to know that He always has His reasons, which are better than mine. Although I admit that I did look for one last thing to put in my cart, I paid and hurried to the car.

Because I had gone to the department store first, the shortest way to the hardware store was through the grocery store parking lot. As I pulled into the lot, a young man, drawers dragging, jumped out of his friend's car and ran into the store. His wallet fell out of his pants right in front of my car!

I hopped out, grabbed the wallet, parked my car, and chased him down near the back of the store!

He was shocked, not even knowing that he had lost his wallet! He threw his arms around my neck and said, "Thank God!" "Thank you!" and "God bless you!" over and over!

"Not many people would do that!" he exclaimed.

"Well, I'm a Christian, too!" I replied.

"Yes, Ma'am!" he said, just glowing!

I winked and told him that losing his wallet was a consequence of "drooping drawers."

"Yes, Ma'am," he said. "I'll pull them up right now!" And he did!

Later we saw each other in the parking lot, and he excitedly told his friend, "That's her!"

He waved and called out to me, "God bless you again!"

I told him of my morning prayer and we just praised God together! Praise the Lord for His goodness and the joy of walking with Him!

It's for My Own Good? Really?

Really! We are to take God's discipline seriously. He tells us, "My son, do not make light of the Lord's discipline, and do not lose heart when He rebukes you, because the Lord disciplines those He loves and He punishes everyone He accepts as a son" (Hebrews 12:5–6). Hebrews 12:10 goes on to say that God disciplines us for our good in order that we may share in His holiness. Instead of dismissing or being discouraged about God's discipline, we can remind ourselves, "My Abba (Daddy) Father loves me. This is just proof that God cares about me and has my welfare in mind."

Whether or not we understand the reasons and the goals for discipline, it is usually not much fun! Hebrews 12:11 acknowledges that, "No discipline seems pleasant at the time, but painful. Later on, however, it produces a harvest of righteousness and peace for those who have been trained by it." If we can endure the discomfort of the training process, we will reach our goal of godliness. It will be worth it!

As we reflect on our main Scripture, Hebrews 12:9, (How much more should we submit to the Father of our spirits and live!) we see that it ends with an exclamation point—something that is not seen very often in Scripture. Certainly, if discipline is so emphasized as the main focus of much of this chapter in the Bible, shouldn't we sit up and take notice?

So what should be our response? "Endure hardship as discipline; God is treating you as sons" (Hebrews 12:7). Don't try to squirm out of or run away from hardship. First ask yourself, "What is God, my Heavenly Father, trying to teach me through this difficulty?" You just may learn a valuable lesson!

Discussion Questions

1. Areas where we are being "disciplined" can also be areas of new growth. In what ways do you feel the Lord is helping you to grow?

_____

_____

_____

_____

_____

2. Looking back on your life, what are some ways that you now see the Lord disciplined you for your own good? What are some benefits that you see in your life now from painful discipline in the past?

_____

_____

_____

_____

_____

3. Have you ever had friends like Job's, who accidently gave you bad advice, blaming you, falsely, for the crisis you were going through at the time? How did you handle it?

_____

_____

_____

_____

_____

Don't Grow Weary

Remember that your victory is just around the corner.

Chapter Eight

STRENGTHEN YOURSELF FOR THE RACE

"Therefore, strengthen your feeble arms and weak knees. Make level paths for your feet, so that the lame may not be disabled, but rather healed" (Hebrews 12:12–13).

Training for the Race of Life

The Apostle Paul often compares this Christian life to a race. The starting line is the day we accept Jesus into our hearts. The finish line is when we complete this earthly race, receive the prize for which God has called us, and meet Jesus face to face. The unique thing about this race, though, is that we run the race and train at the same time! There are no "practice runs"! Paul cheers us on in Philippians 3:14, where he describes his own race: "I press on toward the goal to win the prize for which God has called me heavenward in Christ Jesus." In the meantime, as Hebrews 12:12 says, we are to "strengthen our feeble arms and weak knees."

My (Mary Beth's) daughter Christa is a long-distance runner. My husband and I enjoyed watching her run as we cheered her on through many races during her high school and college years. Christa trained hard for her races. She was dedicated to her running schedule, diet, and rest. She explained that training not only maximized performance, but helped to prevent injury as well. She was careful to pay attention to her form, or she could get injured. Not only did Christa run hard, she ran smart!

A Marathon, Not a Sprint

Likewise, our race of life can be full of surprising challenges—more of an arduous, cross-country marathon than a sprint on a well-manicured track! But God's Word coaches us to train for whatever our particular course demands.

In his classic book, The Pilgrim's Progress, John Bunyan presents an allegory which beautifully illustrates this race of life (Bunyan 1628). A man named Pilgrim left his hometown, the City of Destruction, on his way to the King's Celestial City. At one point, Pilgrim was terrified for his life, so he exclaimed, "What must I do to be saved?" A man named Evangelist appeared along the path and showed him the way to go.

Along the way, Pilgrim encountered many other travelers. Some even joined him as he passed through the Slough of Despond, the worldly city of Vanity Fair, and the dungeon of Doubting Castle belonging to the Giant of Despair. His good friend, Faithful, was martyred along the way, but another good friend, Hopeful, joined him on the journey and remained with him until the end. Pilgrim and Hopeful faced many trials throughout their travels. Pilgrim's final obstacle was the Dark River. He was almost overcome by the waters, but Hopeful helped him to the other side where they were gloriously welcomed into the Celestial City!

Like Pilgrim, as we encounter life's obstacles it is important to remember that we do not travel alone! We are part of a team. At times we may require help just to carry on. At other times we will be the one called upon to lend a hand. But as we trust God, He will always provide exactly what we need.

Run the Race.

Sometimes we may feel so weighed down with things we think God is asking us to do that we can barely walk, much less run! When we feel overwhelmed, it's good to remember that God actually wants us to cast our cares on Him, not the other way around! This overly-burdened feeling might actually be a result of messages we received from our earthly fathers rather than our Heavenly Father.

Research shows that when learning "goodnight prayers," young children are actually thinking, "Dear Heavenly version of my earthly father…" I (Dr. Meier) have done research with hundreds of my seminary students and have found that this is often (though not always) true. They all believed the Bible, but many had doubts in their gut about God in areas where their father or mother were weak.

With our clients who call themselves atheists, I have found that most had an absent father—or a father they wish had been absent! I surprise them by saying that I don't want to talk about God with them—just about their fathers. When they resolve the conflicts with their absent fathers, many have a breakthrough and trust Christ. Strict Dad? Strict view of God. Sugar-Daddy father who spoils you and gives you whatever you want? Disillusionment when God doesn't do things your way. Overwhelmed with too many things God is asking you to do? Wrong!! His yoke is easy and His burden is light. So if you are feeling overly taxed, consider that you may be doing too much. You may need a counselor or a Growing Stronger Group to help you learn ways to eliminate much of your stress.

Remember what we said earlier—pray for God to lighten your load whenever possible, but also to strengthen your back when the load seems overwhelming. God will never give you more than you can handle. 1 Corinthians 10:13 promises, "No temptation has overtaken you except what is common to mankind. And God is faithful; He will not let you be tempted beyond what you can bear. But when you are tempted, He will also provide a way out so that you can endure it."

So Where are We Going, Anyway?

In every one of Christa's cross country races, officials had arrived early and marked out the course. Runners were led through a pre-race walk-through so that they knew the route. They learned where the course wound and where the hills and obstacles were. Not only did this help them stay on course, but they learned where the finish line was! Runners were able to envision the finish line while pacing themselves to complete the course.

Similarly, we must know where we are running or we will get nowhere fast! In Habakkuk 2:2, God said to "Write down the revelation and make it plain so that the herald may run with it." God's Word sets the course for our race.

Follow God.

So, how do we get there? In order to win this race, we must stay on course. Ephesians 5:1 says to "Follow God's example, therefore, as dearly loved children." While others may think they know a better way to go, Jesus said there is only one way to our Heavenly destination, and that is through Him. The road may be difficult, and at times we may be tempted to follow the crowd on what seems to be an easier route. But Jesus tells us to "Enter through the narrow gate. For wide is the gate and broad is the road that leads to destruction and many enter through it. But small is the gate and narrow the road that leads to life, and only a few find it" (Matthew 7:13–14). Jesus is the Gate and Jesus is the only Way!

We need to be on our guard for those who would lead us off course. In Luke 21:8, Jesus warns us not to be fooled by them: "Watch out that you are not deceived. For many will come in My name, claiming, 'I am He,' and, 'The time is near.' Do not follow them." We need to take His route, as Psalm 119:32 says, "I run in the path of Your command, for You have broadened my understanding."

Pace Yourself.

In cross country, Christa described something called finding your "race pace"—that is, during training, finding the kind of pace you'd expect from yourself in order to complete a race. A common error for new runners is to run so fast in the first leg of the race that they are unable to sustain the pace, and they get passed up by other runners in the end.

We also must learn to pace ourselves so that we can avoid burnout and finish strong in the race of life. This is difficult for some hard-driving personalities to accept, but if God rested one day during Creation, perhaps we would be wise to take note and learn from His example! If we don't, we may disqualify ourselves from the race. Christa sadly told of one very athletic teammate who suffered a stress fracture in her foot, apparently from overuse. After that, she was not expected to be able to run competitively again. We need to pace ourselves so that we can stay in the race!

While the Old Testament Jews practiced a strict weekly Sabbath, Hebrews 4 tells us that there is a rest for the people of God who "rest" in the finished work of Jesus Christ on the cross. Verse 11 tells us to "labor" to enter into that rest! So, ironically, our real work is to find our rest in Jesus' finished work, not our own!

Be Careful Not to be Disqualified!

A good coach will work with his or her team to make sure that they know the rules of the race. Training may seem strict, but it's all in the runner's best interest. The coach's goal is to help the runner become the very best athlete he or she can be—and not be disqualified along the way!

Paul put it this way: "But I discipline my body and bring it into subjection, lest, when I have preached to others, I myself should become disqualified" (1 Corinthians 9:27, NKJV). Another version of this verse says, "I strike a blow to my body and make it my slave so that after I have preached to others, I myself will not be disqualified for the prize"(NIV). Still, another says, "I keep under my body, and bring it into subjection: lest that by any means, when I have preached to others, I myself should be a castaway" (KJV).

Strong words! Come on, Paul! Is it really necessary to be that hard on yourself? Isn't that a bit harsh? Actually, Paul knew the truth that "nothing good dwells in me, that is, in my flesh. For I have the desire to do what is right, but not the ability to carry it out" (Romans 7:18, ESV).

Everyone who has ever lived in a human body (except Jesus) has, in one way or another, succumbed to the temptations of "the flesh." That's why Galatians 5:16–17 encourages us to "Walk by the Spirit, and you will not gratify the desires of the flesh." Paul knew that "the flesh desires what is contrary to the Spirit and the Spirit what is contrary to the flesh. They are in conflict with each other, so that you are not to do whatever you want." It is dangerous to do whatever our "flesh" wants! If we do, we will certainly get off course and may even be in danger of being disqualified!

Christa tells me that when running the mile race, the third lap is always the hardest. After two laps around, generally the runner begins to feel tired. It is precisely when the runner is most tired that she needs to surge, making a special effort to run the third lap faster than the first two. She does this because she knows that in the fourth and final lap, the inspiration of being able to see the finish line will allow her to draw from inner resources and sprint the last leg of the race.

In our race, nothing is more heartbreaking than the "fall" of a Christian leader who is nearing the "last lap" of their race. So close to the finish line, they somehow lose focus and yield to temptation they may have resisted countless times before. Even during the writing of this chapter, I have been greatly grieved to hear of such a situation. Like King David and his tryst with Bathsheba, one can be deceived to think that a hidden, brief indulgence may be harmless and inconspicuous. In reality, however, it has the potential to throw thousands off course and cause repercussions for generations to come.

Before we recoil in shock at such devastation, Galatians 6:1 reminds us to gently restore such a person while remaining vigilant that we do not also fall into the same temptation. We are all vulnerable! We must not give up when we get weary, but rely on God's strength to cross the finish line!

Run with Courage!

In 1992, after years of training, Derek Redmond arrived at the Olympic Summer Games in Barcelona with dreams of winning a medal in the 400 meter race. Derek's father Jim, a tremendous encouragement to his son, had traveled to Barcelona to cheer him on. The father and son were very close. Jim had sacrificed much to support Derek's training and growth into an Olympic-class runner (Weinberg n.d.).

The day of the race, Jim found a seat with a view high atop the bleachers in Olympic Stadium. Before a cheering crowd of 65,000 fans, Derek took the lead in the 400 meter race. But only 175 meters away from the finish line, Derek's right hamstring suddenly popped! Immediately in excruciating pain, Derek fell to the track, clutching his right leg.

Medical personnel with stretchers rushed to the scene, but Derek would have none of it! Struggling to his feet he yelled, "No, there's no way I'm getting on that stretcher. I'm going to finish my race." Then, though the other runners had already completed the race, Derek began to hobble on one foot toward the finish line! The astounded audience rose to its feet with thunderous cheers!

Derek's father tore through the crowd and sped to his son's side. Fiercely determined, he would not be deterred by anyone! With security guards chasing behind, Jim ran to his son and cried, "You don't have to do this!" But seeing Derek's tearful, pain-gripped resolution and with 120 meters yet to go, Jim wrapped his arm around Derek's waist and said, "I'm here, son. We'll finish together." Derek hugged his father's neck and sobbed.

Arm in arm amid the roaring crowd, Derek and his father finished the race together! A few feet from the finish line, Jim let go so that Derek could actually cross the finish line by himself.

Sobbing along with the entire Olympic crowd, Jim told reporters, "I'm the proudest father alive. I'm prouder of him than I would have been if he had won the gold medal. It took a lot of guts for him to do what he did" (Weinberg).

Though it is true that Derek did not win a medal, his courage and the love of his father thrilled and inspired 65,000 fans and countless enthusiasts around the world. Who better to "help someone up" than one who has suffered such a painful fall? So if you have fallen, allow your Heavenly Father to help you up again. It does no good to continually cry in anguish on the sidelines. Ignore those who would try to get you off the track, and know that while it may appear that your race is over, many are still cheering you on to the finish line! True, it may take time to heal and get back on course, but there is still a race to be run and many others will need your strong arm to help them along the way!

Run in Order to Receive the Prize!

In 1 Corinthians 9:24 Paul asks, "Do you not know that in a race all the runners run, but only one gets the prize? Run in such a way as to get the prize." In order for a runner to win, it is critical for her to think past the finish line. If she is only running toward the finish line, she will start slowing down when she nears it. Quite the opposite, when one runs past the finish line, she will even throw out her chest and lean into the tape with all her might. Many a photo finish race has been won by these few inches!

Another Olympian and Scotland's all-time greatest runner, Eric Liddell, knew what it meant to run in order to win the prize. When being interviewed about his fantastic pace in the 400 meter race he said, "The secret of my success over the 400 meters is that I run the first 200 meters as hard as I can. Then for the second 200 meters, with God's help, I run harder" (Liddell n.d.).

In Olympic races, each runner must have a number. Marathons also typically require a registration and a number unless they allow some athletes to "run bandit." Even so, if a "bandit" runner comes in first place, he would never be considered the official winner. In a marathon, each runner receives his number when he registers. At the end of the marathon, officials use the runner's number to identify him and then call out his name as he crosses the finish line.

In the Christian race, new believers are "registered' in the Lamb's Book of Life when they give their hearts to Jesus. Revelation 2:17 says that at the end of our earthly race, Jesus will give each of us a white stone with a new name written on it. According to Matthew Henry in his commentary on this passage, "This white stone is absolution from the guilt of sin, alluding to the ancient custom of giving a white stone to those acquitted on trial and a black stone to those condemned. The new name is the name of adoption: adopted persons took the name of the family into which they were adopted" (Henry n.d.).

So let's keep running with all our might and all the strength that God gives us. Let's not grow weary and give up, but look past the "finish line" to the prize for which God has called us heavenward in Christ Jesus!

Discussion Questions

1. Describe things that you do that help you "train" for the race you are running.

_____

_____

_____

_____

_____

2. Athletes in training must add certain activities or foods while avoiding others. What are you adding or eliminating from your lifestyle to better your race?

_____

_____

_____

_____

_____

3. It can be very encouraging to train with other people. Who would you consider to be on "your team" in this race? In what ways do you support each other?

_____

_____

_____

_____

_____

4. If you could not answer the above question to your satisfaction, consider the importance of developing "teammates". Bible studies, prayer groups, and support groups are a few ways to develop a support system which is so crucial to a successful Christian life. What are some of the resources that you could access to develop your support system?

_____

_____

_____

_____

_____

Remember That God is On Your Side

God's love is not based on your performance, but on His goodness.

Chapter Nine

THE LORD IS FOR YOU!

"The Spirit of the Lord is on me…to proclaim the year of the Lord's favor and the day of vengeance of our God."
(Isaiah 61:2)

How Much Does God Love Me?

What friend or relative do you love the most? Just think about it—God loves you a million more times than they do! In his book, *God Thinks You're Wonderful*, Max Lucado says, "God is fond of you. If He had a wallet, your photo would be in it. If God had a refrigerator, your picture would be on it. He sends you flowers every spring and a sunrise every morning…Face it, friend. He is crazy about you!" (Lucado 2003).

Well, God did write a Book. And in His Book, He tells how much He loves you. Yes, YOU! "For God so loved the world that He gave His one and only Son, that whoever believes in Him shall not perish but have eternal life" (John 3:16).

Does this sound too good to be true? If you ever doubt it, meditate on Psalm 139. You were fearfully and wonderfully made! When you fell asleep last night, God was thinking about you specifically. When you woke up this morning, He was thinking about you again. The number of times God thinks about you each day is so vast that you can't even count it! With one arm He hugs you and with the other He leads you. He is FOR you! He is there whether it feels that way or not.

God is Paying Attention to You: A Personal Story.

My (Dr. Meier's) life verses, since age sixteen, are Proverbs 3:5–6 about trusting the Lord, acknowledging Him, and letting Him direct your paths. But in 2012, I had a strange experience during Super Bowl week. I had what I like to call one of my "God Dreams." In the dream, He told me to wake up and look up the word "acknowledge." In fifty years, that thought had never occurred to me, so I got a concordance and looked up that particular Hebrew word. It implies recognizing His presence in our lives—often in secret and subtle ways. "Cool!" I thought to myself.

The next day, my wife and I went over to some friends' home for the Super Bowl. I grabbed an old pair of jeans I had not worn for months. When the game was over and I was home changing, a small piece of metal fell out of my blue jeans' pocket. I picked it up, and read the fine-print inscribed on it, "In all your ways acknowledge Him!"

Sometimes, in ignorance, I get angry at God or feel like He's not around. But He reminds us in subtle, and sometimes not so subtle, ways that He is present all around us. He is FOR us. He loves us even when we sin. There is no condemnation.

But I Can't Feel Him There!

Sometimes the effects of past abuse can keep you from "feeling" the presence of God until you work through those memories. Often professional help is needed to do this. The truth is that while we live in this sinful world, whether we feel Him there or not, God is still there! And God is still good! He blesses us daily, sending the rain on the righteous and the unrighteous (Matthew 5:45).

If you struggle with sensing God's love because you can't feel his presence, consider what he sacrificed to express his great love for his children. "For God so loved the world that He gave His one and only Son, that whoever believes in Him shall not perish but have eternal life" (John 3:16).

While this is, obviously, the ultimate loving sacrifice; consider another way that Jesus loves us. In John 13:1 we read that "Jesus knew that the hour had come for Him to leave this world and go to the Father. Having loved his own who were in the world, He loved them to the end". The chapter goes on to describe the beautiful account of Jesus taking the role of a servant and washing the disciples' feet! The King of the Universe stooped low to serve those He loved and asked us to follow His example as we love others.

In the Good Times/In the Bad Times

The problem of pain in this world causes many to think, "So, if God is *for* me, He loves me, and He is thinking about me night and day, then why does He allow bad things in my life?" You may even be tempted to forget or doubt the love and goodness of God when faced with calamities. The truth is that God's love does not exempt you from trials, but in the midst of them you can be assured that God is FOR you. Romans 8:31 says, "What, then, shall we say in response to this? If God is for us, who can be against us?" These very trials, though painful at the time, can strengthen our faith so that we develop perseverance and become mature, not lacking in anything (James 1:3–4).

Consider the words of a friend of Mary Beth's, a beautiful Christian lady named Judy Ilar. She has loved and served Jesus for many years—and she is receiving treatment for cancer. Below is a recent reflection which she posted on Facebook and has graciously shared with us:

> One last round of CHEMOTHERAPY (in 2 weeks). Ever wondered what it's like 2B on chemo?...it's like slow death…ur just laying waiting for ur last breath and would gladly welcome it. What have I learned? That my suffering is nothing compared to what Jesus Christ endured for me in His suffering. I think 'bout His suffering whenever I felt like giving up. He never gave up. He went through it for me. That's why I love my Lord. I now count everything a loss compared to the surpassing greatness of knowing my Lord (Ilar, Facebook 2014).

Judy is a wonderful, joyful person who has walked with the Lord for many years, even serving the Lord as a missionary in civil-war-torn Rwanda. While she has struggled with this illness, she has not made the mistake of blaming God. Rather, Judy knows that God is everything to her and her greatest source of help in time of need.

There are times, however, when, due to the fallen condition of this world, we suffer at the hands of evil people. Psalm 18 tells us that God is outraged at this. Even more sobering are the words of Jesus in Matthew 18:6 regarding those who would dare to harm a child: "But if anyone causes one of these little ones who believe in me to sin, it would be better for him to have a large millstone hung around his neck and to be drowned in the depths of the sea."

God is very concerned about justice, but don't be confused when His timetable may differ from ours. "Vengeance is mine, I will repay, says the Lord" (Romans 12:19). One day God will settle accounts with those who have injured others. We are not to take matters into our own hands. To the contrary, "if your enemy is hungry, feed him; if he is thirsty, give him something to drink; for by so doing you will heap burning coals on his head. Do not be overcome by evil, but overcome evil with good" (Romans 12:20–21).

Blessed, Even In Persecution

There are also times when we suffer for righteousness' sake. In these cases, Jesus says that we are blessed because we are suffering as He did. In such times, you should not be "surprised at the painful trial you are suffering, as though something strange were happening to you. But rejoice that you participate in the sufferings of Christ, so that you may be overjoyed when His glory is revealed" (1 Peter 4:12–13). We *can* entrust ourselves to our faithful Creator (1 Peter 4:19) and know that He will make everything right.

You may wonder, "If bad things happen to good people, is there nothing that I can do about it?" Yes, there is! Early in the history of man, God made it clear that our choices can play a role in many of the twists and turns of life. God tells us in Deuteronomy 28 that we can choose either blessing or cursing on our lives. If we choose to obey His commands, we are choosing life for us and our descendants.

What about My Bad Choices?

Unfortunately, sometimes we may suffer as a result of our own unwise choices. The law of sowing and reaping applies here. Even so, our amazing God of grace is full of mercy and, like the Father of the prodigal son, He runs to receive us back when we come to Him in repentance.

When my (Mary Beth's) children were young, I made up several little ditties that I used to sing to them. My daughter Bethany, now a grown woman with a child of her own, surprised me one day when she told me how much this little song meant to her:

> I love you when you're good,
> I love you when you're bad,
> I love you when you're happy,
> I love you when you're sad,
> No matter what you do,
> No matter what you say,
> You're still my little Bethany,
> I love you anyway!

Although I was careful not to say, "You're naughty!" or "You're bad!" when correcting my children's behavior, there were times, she said, when she knew she had done something wrong and felt very badly about her choices. She would rehearse this little song in her mind and remind herself, "Mommy still loves me!" Today that daughter thrives on introducing people to the love, grace, and forgiveness of Almighty God.

So, whether you are brand new to this experience of knowing God or have known Him for many years, when troubles come, as they will for all of us, don't make the mistake of blaming God. Remember that He is FOR you. Turn *toward*, not *away* from Him. Psalm 46:1 says that He is our refuge and strength, our ever-present help in trouble. He truly will work ALL things together for our good,

Discussion Questions

1. The passing of time can give us a perspective on suffering that we cannot have when we are in the middle of it. Can you describe a situation that was difficult at the time, but which God later turned around for good?

_____

_____

_____

_____

2. When we suffer unjustly, it can be tempting to retaliate. Jesus showed us a better way when He instructed us to turn the other cheek (Matthew 5:39). This is so contrary to human nature because we fear we will be injured further. In such cases, Jesus is our example again. He said in John 10:18 regarding His own life, "No one takes it from me, but I lay it down of my own accord." This does not mean that we subject ourselves to abuse. It is important to take the necessary steps to be safe. What it does mean is that we do not return evil for evil, but with blessing (1 Peter 3:9). Take a moment to discuss the application of these Scriptures in your life.

_____

_____

_____

_____

3. One of the reasons it can be so difficult to return good for evil is that, in our finite thinking, we fear that justice will not be done. In such cases, 1 Peter 4:19 urges us to commit ourselves to our faithful Creator and continue to do good. We are to leave the injustice of the situation with God and trust that He will heal our souls. Psalm 96:13 says, "He comes to judge the earth: He shall judge the world with righteousness, and the people with His truth." And He will do a much better job than we ever could! Genesis 18:25 says, "Shall not the Judge of all the earth do right?" If you are struggling with such a situation, pause now and prayerfully commit this concern to the Lord.

_____

_____

_____

_____

_____

Do Not Grieve Alone

Weep with those who weep until God, Himself, wipes away all your tears.

Chapter Ten

TO COMFORT ALL WHO *MOURN*

"The Spirit of the Lord is on me…to comfort all who mourn, and provide for those who grieve in Zion—to bestow on them a crown of beauty instead of ashes, the oil of gladness instead of mourning, and a garment of praise instead of a spirit of despair."
(Isaiah 61:2b–3)

I Know that God Sees Everything, but Does He Care?

God does care when we hurt. He knows that we need His help when we grieve. God doesn't tell us to be brave and stop crying when we are hurting. Instead, as a loving Father, He pays very close attention to how we feel. Psalm 56:8 says, "You've kept track of my every toss and turn through the sleepless nights, each tear entered in your ledger, each ache written in your book" (The Message).

Jesus Can Relate!

John 11 tells the story of three siblings, Mary, Martha, and Lazarus who were close friends of Jesus. But just because they were close to Jesus did not mean that they would escape sorrow in this life. While Jesus was in another town, Lazarus became deathly ill. Having seen Jesus perform many miracles, Mary and Martha knew that Jesus could help their brother. They sent word for Jesus to come, but knowing that He intended to raise Lazarus back to life, Jesus purposely delayed until after Lazarus had died.

When Jesus arrived, He was greeted by Lazarus' sisters and a group of people in mourning. Even though He knew that the situation was only temporary, He was very sad. He did not tell Mary, Martha, and the rest of the mourners to stop crying, but empathized with them and entered into their grief. John 11:33–36 tells us, "When Jesus saw her (Mary) weeping, and the Jews who had come along with her also weeping, He was deeply moved in spirit and troubled." Jesus wept, too.

Greg Laurie, in his book, *Hope for Hurting Hearts*, points out that when Jesus was moved in spirit and troubled, the Greek word for "troubled" could actually be translated as "angry" (Laurie 2008). Why would Jesus be sad when He knew that He would raise Lazarus from the dead? And why would Jesus be angry that Lazarus had died when He had purposely stayed away long enough for Lazarus to go through the dying process?

I believe it is because Jesus sympathizes with us. Because He left Heaven and lived as a human, Hebrews 4:15 says that He is touched with the feeling of our weaknesses and infirmities. He is affected with the very same feelings that we feel when we encounter sickness and death, so He can have compassion on us. It is normal to feel sad and angry when someone we love is taken from us through death. Jesus is *all God*, and He is *all man* too! So He also felt sad and angry at the death of His friend.

Jesus also loved and cared for Mary, Martha, and Lazarus as their friend and their Savior. He wasn't just an acquaintance. He knew them well as a human being and as their God. They knew the details of each other's lives.

Amazingly, in John 15:15, Jesus, the Son of God, says that He no longer calls us servants, but friends! He says that a servant does not know his master's business, but whatever He has received from the Father, He now has made known to us! Jesus knows and cares about the details of our lives, and through the Holy Spirit in our hearts, we can know Him and His plans too!

But always the Teacher, Jesus was not only empathizing, He was modeling how to be present with and love those who are grieving. He was showing us how to weep with those who weep. He was saying, "It is ok to be angry, to be sad, and to cry when you lose a loved one." He didn't rebuke Martha and Mary when they blamed Him for letting their brother die because of His absence. He also didn't jump to fix the situation, but first confirmed that He cared about and understood their emotions.

Beyond the interactions with these sisters, Jesus was also affirming to men and women, everywhere and for all time, that it is alright for men to cry. God knows that men need the emotional expression of tears as much as women do, and that crying does not make one less manly. Jesus held the power of life and death in a single word, yet He openly allowed others to see His tender heart expressed through tears.

But once Jesus demonstrated His presence, love, and empathy, He didn't stop there. He proved, as He said in John 11:25–26, that He IS the resurrection and the life. Anyone who believes in Jesus, though he dies, he shall live! Also, anyone who lives and believes in Jesus shall never die. In raising Lazarus from the dead, Jesus not only gave Lazarus back his earthly life, but proved that Jesus is the one who holds the power over death! He will give eternal life to those who die believing in Him.

How Does God Comfort Us?

God is love. God understands that we need comfort! Isaiah 53 shows how Jesus identifies with our grief. Here, He is called the "Man of Sorrows." It says that He was acquainted with grief. Not only did He take our sins upon the cross, but Isaiah goes on to say that He bore our grief and carried our sorrows! He cares deeply when we are affected by the loss of a loved one, the loss of a dream, or something significant in our lives. He knows us better than anyone else and promises to comfort us just as a mother or father would comfort their hurting child. Isaiah 66:13 says, "As a mother comforts her child, so will I comfort you." Who can bring more consolation to a child than her mother? Yet, we also have a deep need for fatherly love. God has promised, "As a father has compassion on his children, so the Lord has compassion on those who fear Him; for He knows how we are formed, He remembers that we are dust" (Psalm 103:14).

Again, Jesus expressed motherly love when He said, "How often I have longed to gather your children together, as a hen gathers her chicks under her wings" (Matthew 23:37). Just like a mother hen, Jesus longs to cover us with His wings and bring us comfort and safety from the inevitable storms of life. Again, Psalm 91:4 says, "He will cover you with

His feathers, and under His wings you will find refuge; His faithfulness will be your shield and rampart."

Ultimately, God will personally wipe away every tear from our eyes. There will be no more death or mourning or crying or pain, for the old order of things (the world as we know it now) will have passed away (Revelation 21:4). But for now, the Holy Spirit, who is actually called "The Comforter," comforts our hearts in the middle of our grief and sorrow. After we have received that comfort, He then asks us to pass on the comfort which we have received to others.

Don't Grieve Alone!

Just as Jesus wept with Mary and Martha, He knows that our painful journey of grief is not to be traveled alone. We need other people to come alongside us as we work through the emotions surrounding loss. Jesus did this with His friends. He will help us too! Mourning, which is the outward expression of grief, brings our sorrow into relationship with God and others.

An important part of the ministry of Jesus is "to comfort all who mourn and to provide for those who grieve" (Isaiah 61:2–3a). Because we are the Body of Christ on this Earth, we also have received this commission to comfort others. People experiencing grief and sorrow need the emotional support and practical care of Christ through us! The "God of all comfort" consoles us, then "we can comfort those in any trouble with the comfort we ourselves have received from God. For just as the sufferings of Christ flow over into our lives, so also through Christ, our comfort overflows" (2 Corinthians 1:4–5).

This giving and receiving of comfort increases bonding and love between people. As Jesus said, "Blessed are those who mourn, for they will be comforted" (Matthew 5:4). God blesses those who mourn as He brings them comfort. Likewise, rather than telling someone, "Don't cry," we can share in the compassion of Christ as we bring comfort to others. When we do this, we are fulfilling the scriptural command to "Rejoice with those who rejoice, and weep with those who weep" (Romans 12:15).

How Long Will it Take?

When we are in the middle of grief, it can be hard to imagine that happy days will ever come again. Though it may not seem like it at the time, little by little, joy *will* return. While depression can come and sit like a gray cloud, the process of grief *does* have an end. Isaiah 57:18 says, "I have seen his ways, but I will heal him; I will guide him and restore comfort to him." Jeremiah 31:13 says, "I will turn their mourning into gladness; I will give them comfort and joy instead of sorrow."

Also, Jeremiah 31:3–4 says that the Lord loves us with an everlasting love and draws us with His unfailing kindness. Because of this, in time we will once again "go out to dance with the joyful".

We Do Not Grieve as Others Do.

Though Christians are subject to the hardships and losses that come with living on planet Earth, we do not grieve as others do who have no hope! Because Jesus died and rose again, we know that we too will rise to live forever in Heaven with Him! Although death causes great pain, Jesus' resurrection and our promised resurrection to eternal life takes away death's sting!

Testimony from Mary Beth

My father, Rev. John M. Baker, was a very special and beloved man. A Free Methodist pastor for over fifty years, he was highly esteemed by thousands of people. But to me, he was Daddy and my hero! He lived and loved in such a way as to exemplify the heart of my loving Heavenly Father.

When Dad passed away at age eighty, family and friends flew in from all over the country to honor his life. Although my family grieved greatly, we discovered that death had lost its sting.

During the process of helping my mother with memorial arrangements, some of my family members, along with Mom and Dad's pastor, gathered at the funeral home in the room where Dad's body lay. It was now only a shell of the man that we all loved so much. His spirit was with Jesus! Yes, there were tears, but because we are also a very musical family, someone began to lead out in a song of worship. All of us, including my mother, the grieving widow, held hands and sang song after song of praise and thanks to God, many of which we had sung with our father (a wonderful tenor!). We stopped singing only because we realized that we might have been too loud and joyful for the people who were visiting in other rooms! Then the pastor led the family in a wonderful prayer before we each said our tender and tearful good-byes.

This type of rejoicing in the middle of sorrow is only possible through the power of the Holy Spirit and the knowledge that the loved one is now in the arms of Jesus!

Pass it On!

Because we do have hope and consolation from the Holy Spirit, we can pass this comfort on to those around us who have also suffered loss. Here are seven practical suggestions—possibly, one for every day of the week—to help others who are grieving:

1. Respond with a phone call, card, or letter. The mourner may treasure these written notes for a long time.
2. Don't worry if you don't know what to say. Many times your very presence, a hug, or a shared tear is enough to express that you care. "Weep with those who weep" (Romans 12:15).

3. Reassure the mourner that grieving is a necessary part of her recovery. Remind her that she may need support for months to come because grieving takes time.
4. Listen compassionately as she expresses her thoughts and feelings.
5. Don't be afraid to talk about the deceased loved one, but share encouraging memories.
6. Don't say, "Let me know if there's anything I can do." Offer specific, practical assistance for daily needs and duties which can overwhelm a grieving person.
7. Assure her of your continual prayer support. Make yourself available for a visit or phone call to pray with her when she feels the need.

Grief is a process with a beginning and an end. While things will never be the way they were before the loss, she will find a "new normal" and feel happiness and joy once again. Weeping may endure for the night season, but Psalm 30:5 assures us, "rejoicing comes in the morning"!

Discussion Questions

1. A Honduran proverb says, "Grief shared is half grief; joy shared is double joy." God knows that we need others when we are grieving, which is why Romans 12:15 says, "Rejoice with those who rejoice; mourn with those who mourn." If you are experiencing grief right now, don't do it alone. With whom can you share this grief and how?

_____

_____

_____

_____

_____

2. Consider joining a support group to process your grief. Christian support groups, such as GriefShare, meet in many churches across the country. Don't be alone, but be proactive and check the internet for resource groups that meet near you.

_____

_____

_____

_____

3. In order to grieve in a healthy way, we need to understand what the loss involves. Each loss will have multiple levels. For example, losing a job involves not only the loss of income, but a secondary loss of the daily camaraderie of co-workers.

   The following is a huge assignment, so take it slowly, and, if at all possible, do it together with someone you trust. If you are currently suffering a loss or have a loss from the past that you have not worked through, first identify the primary loss, then list the secondary losses associated with it.

_____

_____

_____

_____

4. Describe your pain and share it honestly with God now, and, when possible, with trusted friends. Remember, "Blessed are those who mourn, for they will be comforted"(Matthew 5:4).

_____

_____

_____

_____

_____

Let Your Light Shine

*Allow your crisis to grow you stronger and
MORE equipped to be a blessing to others.*

Chapter Eleven

YOUR FREEDOM BRINGS GOD GLORY

*"They will be called oaks of righteousness,
a planting of the LORD for the display of His splendor."*
(Isaiah 61:3b)

You Will be Called Oaks of Righteousness

I will be called an "Oak of Righteousness"? Is that a compliment? Yes, it's true! Like the wood of an oak tree, beautiful and functional, God will make us magnificent and strong to be used by Him. As Ephesians 2:10 says, "We are God's workmanship, created in Christ Jesus to do good works, which God prepared in advance for us to do."

What an honor to think that by allowing. Jesus to live through me, I can become a "planting of the Lord," a beautiful tree in His garden, which brings Him glory! Isaiah 61:11 describes God's garden: "For as the soil makes the sprout come up and a garden causes seeds to grow, so the Sovereign LORD will make righteousness and praise spring up before all nations."

Beautified Through Brokenness

"But how can I be beautiful and functional?" you may ask. "I've been broken!"

To answer your question, consider the Japanese art of repairing pottery called Kintsugi, which traces back to the fifteenth century. Translated into English, it means "golden joinery" or "to patch with gold." Broken fragments of pottery or china, which otherwise would have been discarded, are rejoined with gold and transformed into uniquely beautiful and valuable works of art! The result is that the repaired pottery is even more beautiful than if it had never been broken (Pottery n.d.).

Years ago, at a ladies' retreat where Mary Beth led worship, a woman who had suffered much in a difficult marriage and with wayward children shared that during worship and prayer, God showed her a mini vision of her heart. It had been broken into many pieces. Then she saw the pieces of her heart put back together again—but this time, God, like a divine Kintsugi artist, had filled the broken places with pure gold! He had beautifully repaired her heart in a way that no one else could!

God is a Potter!

Isaiah 64:8 describes God as a Potter. "Yet You, Lord, are our Father. We are the clay, You are the Potter; we are all the work of Your hand."

Sometimes we may not be thrilled at the Potter's choices, but as Isaiah 29:16 questions, "How foolish can you be? He is the Potter, and He is certainly greater than you, the clay! Should the created thing say of the One who made it, 'He didn't make me'? Does a jar ever say, 'The potter who made me is stupid'?" (NLT). Or as the Message Bible states, "You have everything backward! You treat the Potter as a lump of clay. Does a book say to its author, 'He didn't write a word of me'? Does a meal say to the woman who cooked it, 'She had nothing to do with this'?"

How foolish it would be to respond to God in that way! So even though we may not appreciate brokenness, we can remind ourselves that God knows what He is doing. He truly does work everything together for our good (Romans 8:28). He forms and re-forms us, creating something even more valuable than the original.

Victim No More, but Overcomer!

In Chapter 9, we told about Judy, who was facing her last round of chemotherapy. Listen to what this beautiful woman has to say after completing her treatments:

> I cry more these days…not cuz I'm sad or having a difficult time…I'm just so grateful to the Lord…this journey is not over, but as I look back, I only see God. I see my Father who loves me. I see my Jesus who showed me the true meaning of patient endurance and perfect obedience through His suffering which produced eternal life. I have more clarity today…of what is really important. Truth is, God freed my heart. The world has no hold on me. What the world says is important, is not important to

me. What the world fears, I do not fear. That's real freedom and happiness. It is what it is in this physical, material world. This is not my home. I have my own mansion in Heaven. It's still under construction and that's why I am still here...You too have a mansion in Heaven...Jesus promised. I believe Him. I have only one purpose...love people (Ilar, Facebook 2014).

Judy is not only surviving, she is thriving—in her soul and spirit—as she faces physical challenges with Jesus by her side! Rev. 12:11 declares, "And they overcame him (the devil) by the blood of the Lamb and by the word of their testimony"! Jesus has provided the power to overcome through His death at Calvary, but in order to be an overcomer, we must add our word to His Work! Judy knows that it takes BOTH!!!!

No Big Surprise

Jesus warned us that we would have troubles in this world, but with God's help, as we grow through trials, we can become stronger than ever before. This is not the case with everyone, however. We have a choice about how we respond to suffering. Some people blame God and turn their backs on Him when trials come. Instead of improving through adversity, they often become bitter and resentful.

In 1 Peter 4:12–16, 19, the Apostle Peter describes God's way to view suffering:

Dear friends, do not be surprised at the fiery ordeal that has come on you to test you, as though something strange were happening to you. But rejoice inasmuch as you participate in the sufferings of Christ, so that you may be overjoyed when His glory is revealed. If you are insulted because of the name of Christ, you are blessed, for the Spirit of glory and of God rests on you. If you suffer, it should not be as a murderer or thief or any other kind of criminal, or even as a meddler. However, if you suffer as a Christian, do not be ashamed, but praise God that you bear that name.

So according to Peter, we can face trials with a winning attitude when we remember:

- to not be surprised
- to rejoice that we participate in the sufferings of Christ
- to be overjoyed when Jesus' glory is revealed
- to be blessed when insulted for the name of Christ
- to know that the Spirit of glory and God rests upon us
- to not be ashamed
- to praise God that we bear His name

To Know Him

Previously, I (Mary Beth) described the horrific attack that I suffered by a would-be rapist (see the "Welcome" section). After the attack, I was offered assistance by a Victim's Advocate through the state Prosecuting Attorney's office. While I appreciated the offer and needed the help, I was quick to clarify, "I may have been victimized, but I am *not* a victim! I am an *overcomer!*"

Prior to the attack, I had been meditating on Philippians 3:8–11 and making these verses my prayer to God:

> Yet indeed I also count all things loss for the excellence of the knowledge of Christ Jesus my Lord, for whom I have suffered the loss of all things, and count them as rubbish, that I may gain Christ and be found in Him, not having my own righteousness, which is from the law, but that which is through faith in Christ, the righteousness which is from God by faith; that I may know Him and the power of His resurrection, and the fellowship of

His sufferings, being conformed to His death, if, by any means, I may attain to the resurrection from the dead.

"The fellowship of His sufferings," I thought. "How can I ask Him to provide all my daily needs and yet not be willing to know Him in the fellowship of His sufferings? Am I only a fair-weather follower of Christ? Not THY will but MINE be done? Must Jesus suffer alone while I expect to live a life of ease at His expense?"

These Scriptures broke my heart.

"No! I don't want to be a 'gimme' Christian. I want to be a 'give You all I've got' Christian! I want to KNOW You, Lord, even if it means in the fellowship of Your sufferings, I want to know You *deeply!* I want to know Your heart!" Little did I know that very soon I would experience what it meant to share in the fellowship of His sufferings AND the power of His resurrection!

On the day of the attack, I happily served dinner to our first-time guest who would, unbeknown to us, violently assault me just a few hours later. I was working joyfully as I prepared the meal for someone who did not have the ability to repay me. As I cooked, I said, "This is for You, Jesus! I love You, Jesus!"

The congenial stranger our family entertained for the evening waited for an opportunity to get me alone and then turned monstrous. Though God miraculously helped me to escape, the unthinkable happened. This young man fiercely and relentlessly strangled me.

I felt my spirit floating upward and leaving my body. Suddenly, the faces of my husband and four children passed before me as if in a picture frame. I saw my youngest son who had some physical challenges. I said, "God, Stevie still needs a Mommy!" I felt that I was being cradled in the arms of Jesus. I saw a grassy field with a bright light at the horizon. From beyond the horizon, I could hear heavenly music. It was too far away to distinguish any melody, but I had the sense that it was the combined voices of thousands upon thousands of people worshipping God.

I thought, "Next I'll be in the arms of Jesus. And that's O.K., God, because if You are taking me to Heaven, that means that You will take care of my children too."

As soon as that thought crossed my mind, I was immediately wide-awake! The attacker was right there, staring at me! I ordered him to leave, and he did!!! I immediately called 911 and was taken to the hospital.

The emergency room doctor, alarmed and angry, said he could see broken blood vessels all over my face from ten feet away as he walked into the room. He exclaimed that he had never seen so many broken blood vessels on the face and eyes of a person that was still alive! "That man meant to do you terrible harm, young lady!" he said. Although he dealt with trauma every day, he was visibly upset, pacing the room and yelling orders to the police officer, insisting that they keep a 24-hour guard around my house until the culprit was found!

Two days later, my husband and I called our former pastor, Anthony Simmons, and asked him to come to our house and pray with our family. We sang and prayed together. Pastor Anthony prayed, "Lord, I pray that while I'm still here, the phone will ring, and it will be the detective calling to say that the man who attacked Mary Beth turned himself in, and that the police have him in custody."

I didn't quite have the courage to pray that prayer, but I was grateful that Pastor Anthony did!

No sooner did we sing the last song, "Praise the Name of Jesus," when the phone rang! It was the police! He had turned himself in! They had him in custody! How we rejoiced together at the miracle we had just witnessed!

This may seem to be the end of an awful ordeal, but, in reality, it was just the beginning of a four-year healing process. It would have been easier for me to crawl into a hole and hide during my recovery period, but I knew that 1 Peter 4:19 says: "So then, those who suffer according to God's will should commit themselves to their faithful Creator and continue to do good." I went back to work a week later.

I did not realize that through this suffering God's glory would shine through me. When I returned to work, a woman I had never met stopped me and asked, "What is it with you? You are just glowing!" She had no idea what I had been through, or that I was still very shaky! But as the Word promises, the Holy Spirit and the glory of God were upon me!

This was also confirmed in the courtroom at the attacker's sentencing. At one point, the judge turned to me and said, "I can't imagine the horror that you went through. Mrs. Woll, you obviously have a lot to offer our community. Please don't stop giving!"

The attacker was sentenced to ten years in prison.

Fourteen years later, we were confronted with him once again. Having completed his prison sentence, plus four years of incarceration due to delays of trial, he was going to be tried for Civil Commitment. The jury had to decide whether they found him to have a mental condition or personality disorder which made him highly likely to reoffend.

I was the Prosecution's first witness. Though it was quite stressful, I knew that God would help me. He certainly did!

As I stepped to the witness stand, I leaned on the Scripture from Luke 12:11–12 (NLT),"When you are brought to trial in the synagogues and before rulers and authorities, don't worry about how to defend yourself or what to say, for the Holy Spirit will teach you at that time what needs to be said." I had promised "to tell the truth, the whole truth, and nothing but the truth," so everyone in the courtroom heard about Jesus that day! I didn't hold back as I spoke openly of the vicious attack and of God's protection. I told how the Holy Spirit had given me courage in the middle of horror. I explained how God sent me back from Heaven to finish raising my family. After the trial, a juror told me that there was not a dry eye in the courtroom.

Even the court reporter, whom the Prosecutor teasingly called "Hard-Hearted Hannah," had tears streaming down her face as she took my testimony at the deposition. Afterward, she came up to me and said, "You are such a wonderful person; I'm so sorry that this happened to you!"

I told her that it was not I, but Jesus *in me*, who was wonderful. Then I was able to give her a word of encouragement. I told her that while people thought she was tough, God wanted her to know that she actually had a very tender heart. She only had a tough exterior in order to do her job; otherwise she would cry through her work all day! She smiled, gave me a hug, and said she was so glad that she got to meet me! This was just one small miracle of many that came from this tragedy.

After the trial when I could freely discuss the case, I posted news of the verdict on Facebook, thanking God for the victory in court. Immediately, I received a message from a friend asking me about the case. The very same moment that I posted, another Christian friend of hers whom I had never met posted thanks to God for a court victory where she had served as a juror!

It was the same case!

Later my husband and I were able to meet this juror and her husband for dinner. She told us that the jury had been tied until she (a legal secretary by vocation) showed them her extensive hand-written notes with specific quotes from expert witnesses! As a result, the jury turned, and the defendant was sentenced, indefinitely, to civil commitment. How the four of us rejoiced together at God's amazing and intricate planning! While this evil attack was not God's doing, He turned it all around for my good and to display His glory!

This Little Light of Mine

When we suffer yet continue to do good, we bring glory to God. Jesus told us not to do good works to be seen by other people as the hypocrites do. When we do good things out of a loving relationship with Jesus, we bring God glory! As John 15:8 says, "This is to my Father's glory, that you bear much fruit, showing yourselves to be My disciples."

In Matthew 5:14–16, Jesus said that we are the light of the world. He doesn't want us to hide that light, but hold it up so that it can give light to other people. He said that we are to let our light shine in such a way that people will see our good deeds and glorify our Father in Heaven. We can shine *for* Him even in the darkest moments of our lives.

But what does it mean to let your light shine for Jesus? Just as the moon reflects the greater light of the sun, Christians reflect the glory of The Son. So let your light shine, not so that people will see how wonderful you are, but so they will see, through your good works, how wonderful God is! As we spend time with Him through the Word, prayer, and fellowship, we will bear fruit as we become more and more like Christ. We will "all reflect the Lord's glory" as we "are being transformed into His likeness with ever-increasing glory, which comes from the Lord, who is the Spirit" (2 Corinthians 3:18).

But What If...

You may be asking, "But what about the one who does not survive such an attack? What about those who don't make it through an illness or accident? What about those who are martyred for their faith in Christ?" Right now there are brothers and sisters in Christ all over the world who are suffering just for being Christians.

There are many in this world who have suffered and continue to suffer much more than I ever have. Some have given their lives for the sake of Christ. How can God work all this together for their good when they have already paid the ultimate sacrifice?

Did God forget about them? Did the Potter make a mistake with the clay?

No! There *is* a God in Heaven who is just, and an eternity before us where He will set all things straight.

Amazing, Compensating Grace

No matter what we experience in life, God has promised that He will never give us more than we can bear—even if that means in the very process of dying! Acts chapter 7 tells the story of the first Christian martyr, Stephen. The Bible reports that his face shone like an angel's. Stephen was able to look into Heaven and saw Jesus standing (not sitting) at the right hand of the Father.

Paul was stoned and left for dead. Many think that it was at this time that he experienced what he described in 2 Corinthians 12, where he was caught up into the third Heaven and shown many magnificent things about which he was not permitted to speak.

In addition to Stephen and, ultimately Paul, many untold numbers have been martyred for Christ. Hebrews 11 says that the world was not worthy of them. Revelation tells us that our righteous God will avenge every one of them. In addition, in Heaven they will receive a special crown of life. The first shall be last and the last shall be first!

God chose to spare me, but had He not, I was completely at peace because of His love and care for me. Had He called me to Heaven, I would have been fine with it and known that He would take care of my family. But He had other plans for me—including my co-authoring this book! As I get to enjoy my husband, children, and now grandchildren, I am so very grateful that He let me stay here for a little while longer. I want to fulfill the purposes for which He kept me on Earth!

Discussion Questions

1. Describe people from the Bible who were transformed and became displays of God's splendor. What were they like "before" and "after"?

_____

_____

_____

_____

_____

2. Have you, or anyone you know, gone through this transformation process? If so, please share the "before" and "after" story.

_____

_____

_____

_____

_____

3. How have the above situations brought glory to God?

_____

_____

_____

_____

_____

4. Perhaps you are in the middle of a significant life trial right now. If so, remember that God has invested the very life of His Son, on your behalf, to bring you through this trial to the other side—for your encouragement and His glory! Consider Romans 8:32, "He who did not spare His own Son, but gave Him up for us all—how will He not also, along with Him,

graciously give us all things?" Take a moment to thank God for His sacrifice of Jesus Christ, then ask Him specifically for the help that you need.

_____

_____

_____

_____

_____

Invest In The Future

When you overcome crises with God's help,
you become an example that will encourage generations to come.

Chapter Twelve

REBUILDING THE GENERATIONS

"They will rebuild the ancient ruins and restore the places long devastated;
they will renew the ruined cities that have been devastated for generations."
(Isaiah 61:4)

Ruins Restored, Devastation Renewed

God is a Master Builder—and Re-Builder—even if the devastation has stood for many generations. The book of Nehemiah is a partial fulfillment of Isaiah 61:4, where God's people, led by Nehemiah, rebuilt the rubble of Jerusalem's walls. But the most thrilling example in modern times is the miracle of the rebirth of Israel as a nation.

In the appendix of my (Dr. Meier's) Bible prophecy novel, *The Third Millennium*, I show some mathematical computations based on predictions made in the Old Testament. These predictions show when Israel would become a nation again after "two days" (meaning two thousand years) of being trampled by Gentiles. The several-hundred-thousand-day-count from Ezekiel and Jeremiah ended on May 14, 1948, the precise date when Israel was restored as a nation! God's Word is so accurate that if someone understood math and Bible prophecy, they could have booked a flight to Israel decades earlier! (Meier 1993).

Sir Isaac Newton spent half of his time studying math and the other half on the Bible, including Bible prophecy. He went so far as to learn Hebrew. He came to some similar conclusions in his writings: God promises to rebuild Israel; unfortunately, they have many troubles yet to come (Heller 2012). In the same way, God promises to rebuild our lives and restore us in areas that have not been fruitful for a long time.

Instead of ruin and devastation, shame and disgrace, God promises a double blessing to those who belong to Him. Not only are we blessed, but we can expect our children and their children to receive His blessing as well: "Their descendants will be known among the nations and their offspring among the peoples. All who see them will acknowledge that they are a people the LORD has blessed" (Isaiah 61:7).

For Generations to Come

How do you want to be remembered? Have you thought about it? Whether or not you are aware of making an impact on those around you,

you certainly are! So why not live purposefully with future generations in mind?

As I (Dr. Meier) mentioned earlier, our rule of thumb in medical school was, "See One, Do One, Teach One." I first learned by watching my professors and other experienced doctors, then practiced with them nearby, then helped other medical students by assisting them with what I had learned. The same principle should apply as we work our way through the crises of life. With God's help and using the Twelve Growing Stronger Guidelines, we can emerge from difficulties stronger than we ever were before. But we should not stop there. We should then pass on the principles we have learned from our own struggles to help our children, our friends, and significant others to grow from the wisdom we have gained. In this way, they will be better equipped to resolve future crises which inevitably crop up for all of us.

When our (Mary Beth's) kids were little, we taught them about tithing by giving them three little cups in which to divide their money. One was labeled, "God," the second, "Save," and the third, "Spend." Recently, when babysitting our son David's children, I was delighted to see three little cups labeled—you guessed it—"God," "Save," and "Spend!"

Some lessons, like this, are specifically taught. Others are simply caught in the process of daily living. Still others may not "sink in" until our grown kids have children of their own. What lessons do you want to pass on to the next generation?

The Most Important Lesson

Of course, the most important thing we can teach the next generation is how to become a Christian! We have come full circle! We must always put first things first. As Paul said in Acts 16:31, "Believe in the Lord Jesus, and you will be saved—you and your household." What good would it do to teach them about this life and ignore the eternal life to come? No! As Joel 1:3 reminds us, "Tell it to your children, and let your children tell it to their children, and their children to the next generation."

Set an Example.

Not only do we share the Gospel with the next generation, but we can live a godly life that will encourage them long after we are gone. Though we may not be aware of it, today's events may be retold by our children, grandchildren, and even great grandchildren yet unborn! What kind of legacy do you want to leave? Whether you have biological children or not, faith in Christ, passed through spiritual children, can greatly impact even more than "us four"! For example, Carmen Harris, godmother to Mary Beth's children, will have many children in Heaven because of the people she has loved, served, and led to faith in Christ all around the world.

When my (Mary Beth's) grandchildren are old enough to hear the story of the attack described in the last chapter, I want them to know how God saved my life and transformed such an awful thing into the impetus to help other women in crisis. I pray that my experience will help bring many, many people to Christ.

In 2003, I attended a prayer meeting where a wonderful lady named Fran Lance prayed for my son Steve and me. Since the prayer was recorded, I was able to transcribe it. Fran did not know me well and did not know about the attack.

I am amazed now at the Lord's timing! As I said in the previous chapter, my recovery took about four years. This prayer was exactly four years and two months (to the day) after the attack. Look at the wonderful encouragement that the Lord gave me as Fran prayed:

Father, we just bless your daughter now in Jesus' name. Thank You, Lord.

The Lord gives me Job 13:15, 'Though He slay me, yet will I hope in Him.' I just see you; you've pulled out all the stops. 'I'm going to follow the Lord no matter what.'

Life has not gone the way you thought it would. The Lord says, 'You have rolled with the punches.' I see you in a boxing ring and you've learned to dodge the blow of a punch. These punches are not from the Lord. He wants you to know that. Sometimes people think, 'The Lord's punishing me.' But the Lord says, 'Daughter, I love you so much.' And no way, no way would He ever, ever cause a battering of any kind, any sort, any punch of life. But He has given man free will, and man's free will has battered you.

But the Lord says, 'Daughter, I have brought gold out of you through it all.' Job 23:1, 'But He knows the way that I take. When He has tested me, I will come forth as gold. My feet have closely followed His steps; I have kept His way without turning aside. I have not departed from the commands of His lips. I have treasured the words of His mouth more than my daily bread.'

And that's how the Lord sees you. And you're coming forth as gold. Gold is refined in the fire. So you didn't settle for the silver. Silver doesn't take as much heat as gold, but you said, 'Lord, I want to go for it. I don't want to just have this silver.' You're going for it.

Psalm 78:3, 'What we have heard and known, what our fathers have told us we will not hide them from their children. We will tell the next generation.' The Lord is saying that as you teach your child, it's going to go on to the next generation too, even the next and the next. So verse 6, 'So the next generation would know them, even the children yet to be born. And they, in turn, would tell their children, and then they would put their trust in God.' So as you put your life into your son or children, the Lord says, 'It will go on to the next generation, even to those unborn, yet.'

Thank You, Lord. We just bless Your daughter. We thank You, Lord, for just healing her wounded heart. And we thank You that You are the Healer. The Bible says that the Lord is close to those who are wounded, brokenhearted, Psalm 147:3, 'He heals the brokenhearted and binds up their wounds. He determines the number of stars and calls them each by name. Great is our Lord and mighty in power. His understanding has no limits.' We bless her in Jesus' name. Amen.

As you can imagine, this was a great blessing and tremendous encouragement! If you also have been refined by fire, I would like to share this prayer blessing with you! Please, take this prayer of encouragement and pray it as your own!

Little Ones to Him Belong.

God cares about our suffering. He watches over us and helps us in the recovery process. But little eyes are watching too! Let's honor God, even in our recovery, so that those who follow will have an example to cheer them on when they face the inevitable trials of life. Of course, we would love to spare our children and grandchildren from trials, but our prayers and example can follow them long after we are gone.

One of our teenage clients shared the story of her parents' divorce when she was very young. Custody was split 50/50 between her mother and father, who had both remarried. It soon became clear that she was not safe or well-cared for when she visited her mother's house.

Among other alarming events, there were times when, at five years old, she was left alone to fend for herself and could not find anything in the house to eat.

Of course, the father and stepmother were extremely concerned and frustrated. After great personal expense and many legal struggles, they finally gained full custody.

She expressed how happy she felt when she was able to permanently stay with her father and stepmother. She said that one house was "bad." The other house was "good." After her father and stepmother gained full custody, she was so relieved that it was "all good"! She felt so free!

Just as this young client experienced, it is the same with our Heavenly Father. In this world, we all have trials and even some suffering. It is just the nature of this world. But Jesus told us not to be worried about this because He is preparing a place in Heaven for those who believe in Him. We're going to live in the Father's House forever! It's all good there!! In John 14:1–3 Jesus said, "Do not let your hearts be troubled. You believe in God; believe also in me. My Father's house has many rooms; if that were not so, would I have told you that I am going there to prepare a place for you? And if I go and prepare a place for you, I will come back and take you to be with me that you also may be where I am."

The Cloud of Witnesses Yet to Come.

Hebrews 11:39–40 speaks of Old Testament heroes, including martyrs, who, while they "were all commended for their faith" did not receive "what had been promised" because "God had planned something better for us so that only together with us would they be made perfect."

We know that Jesus is the One who fulfills the promises of the Old Testament, but amazingly enough, this "perfection" of the Old Testament heroes is not referring to Jesus, but to those of US who will pick up their faith baton and run with it!

But it doesn't even end there! Hebrews Chapter 12 begins with these now-familiar verses: "Therefore, since we are surrounded by such a great cloud of witnesses, let us throw off everything that hinders and the sin that so easily entangles. And let us run with perseverance the race marked out for us."

The incredible thing is that this cloud of witnesses watching our race not only includes these heavenly heroes, it also includes those who will come after us—our children, and grandchildren yet unborn—who hear of our faith-filled, God-empowered lives! Our faithful testimony through trial can give courage to those who follow us—even many generations after we are gone—to persevere through their own trials and do great exploits for God!

Children are Our Arrows!

When I (Mary Beth) was nineteen years old and feeling sad from a major disappointment, my very wise father comforted me with this thought: "When an archer shoots an arrow, the farther back he pulls the bow, the farther the arrow will travel." Although I didn't really understand it at the time, I now see that as Christians we can yield to the Archer who will take what seems to be a setback and use it to "shoot us" farther than we ever would have gone had that setback not occurred.

Psalm 127:4–5 says that children are a reward and a heritage from the Lord. It goes on to say that they are like arrows in the hand of a warrior. As women warriors in a spiritual battle, through our prayers and godly example we can shoot the "arrows" of our biological and spiritual children far into the future to win battles for God's Kingdom!

The heart of this book can be summed up in the great mystery of the Cross recorded in John 12:24–26, which Jesus shared with His disciples just prior to the crucifixion:

Very truly I tell you, unless a kernel of wheat falls to the ground and dies, it remains only a single seed. But if it dies, it produces many seeds. Anyone who loves their life will lose it, while anyone who hates their life in this world will keep it for eternal life. Whoever serves Me must follow Me; and where I am, My servant also will be. My Father will honor the one who serves Me.

In the same way, the sacrifices of our sufferings for Jesus will bear much fruit, not only in our lifetime, but as following generations take courage from our example, they will serve to advance the kingdom of God, bearing thirty, sixty, and even one hundred times more fruit!

Next Generation Blessing

We would like to end this book with a Next Generation Blessing prayer. Feel free to add your personalized requests to this prayer for your biological and/or spiritual children, grandchildren, and those yet to be born!

Dear Father,

We pray a blessing on the generations to follow us. We pray that they will come to know You at a very young age. We pray they will love You and serve You all the days of their lives. We pray that they will grow in wisdom and stature and favor with God and man, just like Jesus did.

We pray that they will tell the next generation of Your praiseworthy deeds, Your power, and the wonders You have done. We pray that they would teach their children Your mighty acts, so the next generation would know about them, even the children yet to be born, and they in turn would tell their children. We pray that they would put their trust in You and would not forget Your deeds but keep your commands.

We pray that when they face trials in life, they will remember that the sufferings they experience in this life are nothing compared to the glory that will be revealed in the next one. We pray that they will stand side by side with us in Heaven praising You for the way that You brought us through, all the while changing us from glory to glory. **And we pray that they will not come alone, but through faith in Christ, will bring many untold numbers of people to Heaven with them!**

In Jesus' name, Amen.

Discussion Questions

1. God's plan is for our children to have a life of blessing and peace, as Isaiah 54:13 says, "All your sons will be taught by the LORD, and great will be your children's peace." If there are areas where your children are not enjoying this peace right now, take a minute to describe this to the Lord and ask Him for the peace He has promised.

_____

_____

_____

_____

_____

2. Proverbs 13:22 says, "A good man leaves an inheritance to his children's children." In this case, we are not just referring to a material inheritance, but a legacy of godliness which will bless generations after us, even those who are yet to be born! It's amazing to think about the impact of our daily lives on so

many others. Reflect on what your parents and grandparents have passed on to you. What do you want to pass on to your children and grandchildren?

_____

_____

_____

_____

_____

3. What about the legacy of those who have never been married or never had children? How can they leave an inheritance to the generations to come? Consider godly women like Mother Teresa of Calcutta and Corrie ten Boom who, through the years, have instructed and mentored millions by their examples of integrity, courage, love, and generosity. If you are not a parent at this time, how would you like to live your life in such a way as to impact future generations?

_____

_____

_____

_____

_____

4. Although we admire heroes of the faith and our culture, none of them were perfect! We do not have to live perfect lives to affect those who follow us. In fact, some of us may best glorify God by telling of His wonderful forgiveness and restoration in our lives, or how He saved us from calamity and disaster. As a final homework assignment of this study, picture your descendants—either your children, grandchildren, or others that your life may touch—and write a letter expressing what

God has done in your life and the legacy you would most want to impart to them.

_____

_____

_____

_____

_____

THE TWELVE
GROWING STRONGER GUIDELINES

1. **Keep First Things First.** Develop an intimate relationship with Jesus, the true Higher Power because you are powerless to overcome crises in your own strength, alone. "The Spirit of the Sovereign Lord is on me, because the Lord has anointed me to preach good news to the poor" (Isaiah 61:1).

2. **Don't Suffer Alone.** Give your broken heart to God and His people to receive healing from both. "The Spirit of the Sovereign Lord is on me... He has sent me to bind up the brokenhearted" (Isaiah 61:1).

3. **Confession Leads to Freedom.** To become truly free from bondage and truly healed, you must confess your own sins and flaws to safe, significant others as well as to Jesus. "The Spirit of the Sovereign Lord is on me ... to proclaim freedom for the captives and release from darkness for the prisoners" (Isaiah 61:1).

4. **With God's Help, Get Rid of It.** Lay aside the things that are holding you back. "Therefore, since we are surrounded by such a great cloud of witnesses, let us throw off everything that hinders and the sin that so easily entangles, and let us run with perseverance the race marked out for us" (Hebrews 12:1).

5. **Keep Looking Up.** Make PERSONAL GROWTH an even higher priority than resolving your current crisis. "Let us fix our eyes on Jesus, the author and perfector of our faith" (Hebrews 12:2a).

6. **Hang In There.** Whenever you feel like giving up, endure. "Jesus…who for the joy set before Him endured the cross, scorning its shame, and sat down at the right hand of the throne of God" (Hebrews 12:2b).

7. **Don't Lose Heart.** When you experience discipline, remind yourself that God is a good Father and say, "My Abba (Daddy) Father loves me." "Moreover, we have all had human fathers who disciplined us and we respected them for it. How much more should we submit to the Father of our spirits and live!" (Hebrews 12:10).

8. **Don't Grow Weary.** Remember that your victory is just around the corner. "Therefore, strengthen your feeble arms and weak knees. Make level paths for your feet, so that the lame may not be disabled, but rather healed" (Hebrews 12:12–13).

9. **Remember That God is On Your Side.** God's love is not based on your performance, but on His goodness. "The Spirit of the Lord is on me…to proclaim the year of the Lord's favor and the day of vengeance of our God" (Isaiah 61:2).

10. **Do Not Grieve Alone.** Weep with those who weep until God, Himself, wipes away all your tears. "The Spirit of the Lord is on me…to comfort all who mourn, and provide for those who grieve in Zion—to bestow on them a crown of beauty instead of

ashes, the oil of gladness instead of mourning, and a garment of praise instead of a spirit of despair" (Isaiah 61:2b–3).

11. **Let Your Light Shine.** Allow your crisis to grow you stronger and MORE equipped to be a blessing to others. "They will be called oaks of righteousness, a planting of the Lord for the display of His splendor" (Isaiah 61:3b).

12. **Invest In The Future.** When you overcome crises with God's help, you become an example that will encourage generations to come. "They will rebuild the ancient ruins and restore the places long devastated; they will renew the ruined cities that have been devastated for generations" (Isaiah 61:4).

MY STORY

Writing can be a wonderful healing tool in the process of recovering from trauma. The following pages are provided for you to write your own Growing Stronger story.

_____

_____

_____

_____

_____

_____

_____

_____

_____

_____

_____

_____

_____

_____

_____

_____

LEADERSHIP TRAINING GUIDE

Growing Stronger Purpose

VISION

To provide training and support for leaders in the local church so that women can offer a place of refuge and healing for other women temporarily experiencing crises, trauma, depression, or grief so that they can recover and return to a life of fruitfulness.

Hopes and Expectations

Where to Turn?

Women experiencing crises, trauma, depression, or grief often feel isolated and don't know where to turn for help. Although the church wants to be a refuge and members of the church want to minister to women in such need, we often don't know how to help. Pastors and staff can become overwhelmed with the volume and intensity of the needs of their congregation, so the cycle of isolation and frustration continues.

Help is Available!

There are women in every church who have a calling from God to help others in crisis, but need training to fulfill that calling. Growing Stronger provides the information, structure, and support necessary for them to facilitate ongoing groups, providing a much-needed safety net to receive and help stabilize women in crisis.

Although Growing Stronger was founded by a licensed therapist, individual groups are not meant to provide counseling, but to supplement counseling and provide a setting where women in crisis can recover and grow in a safe, caring group.

CORE VALUES

Christ's Commission causes us to care for and comfort women in crisis to recover and return to a life which is thirty, sixty, or even a hundred times more fruitful than ever before!

Commission

God calls every Christian to:

- go into all the world;
- make disciples of all nations;
- baptize in the name of the Father, Son, and Holy Spirit, and;
- teach them to obey Jesus' commands.

Then Jesus came to them and said, 'All authority in heaven and on earth has been given to Me. Therefore **go** and **make disciples** of all nations, **baptizing them** in the name of the Father and of the Son and of the Holy Spirit, and **teaching them** to obey everything I have commanded you. And surely

I am with you always, to the very end of the age' (Matthew 28:18–20, emphasis ours).

Cares vs. Crops

God wants our lives to be fruitful.

Cares of this life include:

- crises,
- trauma,
- depression, and
- grief.

These can temporarily disable us and cause us to become unfruitful in the purposes for which we were created.

Still others, like seed sown among thorns, hear the Word, but the worries of this life, the deceitfulness of wealth, and the desires for other things come in and **choke the Word, making it unfruitful.** Others, **like seed sown on good soil, hear the Word, accept it, and produce a crop—thirty, sixty, or even a hundred times what was sown** (Mark 4:18–20, emphasis ours).

Christ's Comfort in Community

Jesus came to comfort us and to set us free.

The Spirit of the Lord is on Me, because He has anointed Me to preach good news to the poor. He has sent Me **to proclaim freedom for the prisoners** and recovery of sight for the blind, **to release the oppressed**, to proclaim the year of the Lord's favor. **To comfort all who mourn, and provide for those**

who grieve in Zion—to bestow on them a crown of beauty instead of ashes, the oil of joy instead of mourning, and a garment of praise instead of a spirit of despair (Isaiah 61:2b–3, emphasis ours).

God wants us to comfort others.

Praise be to the God and Father of our Lord Jesus Christ, the Father of compassion and the God of all comfort, **who comforts us in all our troubles, so that we can comfort those in any trouble with the comfort we ourselves have received from God.** For just as the sufferings of Christ flow over into our lives, so also **through Christ our comfort overflows** (2 Corinthians 1:3–5, emphasis ours).

THE GROWING STRONGER MISSION IN THE GOSPELS

(The Four 4:18–20's)

Matthew 4:18–20: God Calls us to His Commission.
The Calling of the First Disciples

> As Jesus was walking beside the Sea of Galilee, He saw two brothers; Simon called Peter and his brother Andrew. They were casting a net into the lake, for they were fishermen. 'Come, follow Me,' Jesus said, 'and I will make you fishers of men.' At once they left their nets and followed Him.

Mark 4:18–20: Cares of the World can Cause us to be "Out of Commission."
The Parable of the Sower

> Still others, like seed sown among thorns, hear the Word; but the worries of this life, the deceitfulness of wealth, and the

desires for other things come in and choke the Word, making it unfruitful. Others, like seed sown on good soil, hear the Word, accept it, and produce a crop—thirty, sixty, or even a hundred times what was sown.

Luke 4:18–20: We are Anointed to Bring Christ's Comfort.

The Anointing of Jesus upon Us

The Spirit of the Lord is on Me, because He has anointed Me to preach good news to the poor. He has sent Me to proclaim freedom for the prisoners and recovery of sight for the blind, to release the oppressed, to proclaim the year of the Lord's favor.'

Then He rolled up the scroll gave it back to the attendant and sat down. The eyes of everyone in the synagogue were fastened on Him.

John 4:18–20: Jesus Cares for Women who are in Crisis.

The Woman at the Well

Jesus said to her, 'You are right when you say you have no husband. The fact is, you have had five husbands, and the man you now have is not your husband. What you have just said is quite true.'

'Sir,' the woman said, 'I can see that you are a prophet. Our fathers worshiped on this mountain, but you Jews claim that the place where we must worship is in Jerusalem.'

Jesus proceeded to lead her to salvation. As a result of her testimony, many in her village were also saved.

BUILDING A LEADERSHIP TEAM

Growing Stronger is an intensive-care support group ministry within the local church to help women in crisis recover and return to a life that is thirty, sixty, and even a hundred times more fruitful than before!

Growing Stronger Team Structure

Due to the critical needs of the Participants, the structure of the ministry includes a supportive team of four people: 1) the Growing Stronger Leader 2) the Assistant Leader 3) a Professional Counselor and 4) the Pastor, or in some larger churches, the Pastor of Women's Ministries. At times, a Women's Pastor may choose to fill the role of the Growing Stronger Leader herself. In that case, the Senior Pastor would fill the fourth team position. Because this is a ministry by women for women, the Leader, Assistant Leader, and Counselor positions should be held by women.

Before discussing the roles of each team member, we will first provide a context for these roles by describing the format of Growing Stronger groups.

Each weekly Growing Stronger group includes the following elements:

1. The Leader and Assistant Leader meet before group to pray for each other and the needs of the group.
2. The group meets for a meal, preferably in the same home each week.
3. The meal is followed by an ongoing, biblically-based book study taught by the Leader.
4. The Leader facilitates a Participant sharing time.
5. The Leader or Assistant Leader prays for each Participant's needs.
6. The Counselor teaches a chapter from the book, or coordinating lesson, (once a month) and facilitates the group sharing time.

In addition to the weekly meetings, the Counselor and Leader meet once a month for mentoring, debriefing, and prayer support for each other and the group. Also, the Pastor and Leader meet briefly once a week for prayer and to update the Pastor on the progress and needs of the ministry.

The Leader

Becoming a Leader in the Growing Stronger ministry requires one to take on the role of a servant, as Jesus did. Dr. Dan C. Hammer, in his book *Servant Leadership: A Concept That Has Come into Its Own* highlights the fact that a servant is to be involved in:

- **S**erving
- **E**quipping
- **R**elationships
- **V**ulnerability
- **A**ssisting
- **N**urturing
- **T**eaching (Hammer 2012).

A woman in crisis will need others to step in and do what she would normally do for herself until she returns to health and strength. Depending on her situation, this may require emotional, spiritual, and practical support. It is important for the Leader to remember that her role is limited, but critical, in the Participant's recovery journey. The Leader cannot, and must not, try to do everything, but supplies a weekly, consistent, safe, and supportive place for each Participant to receive nurturing, fellowship, teaching, and encouragement.

The Assistant Leader

The role of the Assistant Leader is to come alongside the Leader as a partner to provide her with prayer, encouragement, and practical assistance as needed. The Assistant Leader should also be prepared to lead the Growing Stronger group in the case of the Leader's absence. The Assistant Leader should have the same qualifications as the Leader. Also, the Assistant Leader is in a great position to be mentored by the Leader to start her own Growing Stronger group in the future.

The Counselor

A beautiful and unique feature of the Growing Stronger ministry is the support of a professional Counselor. The specialized training and consultation which the Counselor provides makes it possible for the Leader to care for a group of women with potentially intense life situations. Because the Counselor also facilitates the group once a month, the Leader has the opportunity to observe and learn from the Counselor.

Since the Growing Stronger ministry is soliciting the help of a professional Counselor, it is important to consider compensation, since this is her occupation "A worker deserves (her) wages" (Luke 10:7). This arrangement depends on the wishes of the Counselor and the funds available to the Women's Ministry budget. The Counselor may decide to donate her time as a ministry outreach. Or the church could offer to compensate the Counselor what she would normally be paid for one client hour. Although the Counselor will be spending three to four hours per month with the Growing Stronger ministry, our experience is that this lower fee is affordable for most churches and makes it possible for the Participants to come without charge. Inevitably the Counselor will also receive other referrals from the church, so although she is donating much of her time, it becomes a mutually beneficial relationship.

We realize that a Counselor may not be available in some remote areas. If this is the case, with the Pastor's endorsement, the Leader may search out a qualified, mature Christian woman to fill the Counselor role who has a heart for, and experience with, helping hurting women.

In addition to monthly meetings, it is recommended that the Counselor also meet with the Leader in person once a month to provide support and discuss difficult situations regarding Participants, such as the need for individual counseling or medical treatment.

If, in the course of a Growing Stronger meeting, it becomes apparent that a Participant is in need of professional counseling or psychiatric care, the Leader should refer the Participant to the Counselor who will, in turn, refer her to appropriate professional help.

The Pastor

The Pastor is the spiritual support person for the Leader. His role on the team is to be available to advise, pray with, and encourage the Leader.

The Pastor and church staff may refer a potential Participant to the Leader, who will follow up with her to see if her needs would best be met through a Growing Stronger group. It is recommended that the Leader add members to the group by personal invitation rather than the Pastor's open announcement to the church. This is not meant to be exclusive, but rather to offer group members a safe place to build relationships and bond within a sense of group identity and security.

The Leader explains to the potential Participant that the group is a safe-haven bonding place, rather than an occasional drop-in Bible study. If the Growing Stronger group seems to be a good resource for her, the Leader introduces the new member at the next Growing Stronger group meeting.

There may be times when the Leader will need to refer a member back to the Pastor or church staff for benevolence help or other pastoral assistance beyond the scope of a Growing Stronger group.

QUALIFICATIONS FOR LEADERS

A Leader should have the support of her church's Pastor and/or Women's Ministry Leader. When starting a Growing Stronger group, one should look for Leaders and Assistant Leaders within the local church who possess the important characteristics listed below. These qualities will help their effectiveness with Participants and protect Leaders and Assistant Leaders from potential problems (Tan 1991).

A Mature Christian
Because the Leader will assist Participants through major life challenges, it is important that she have a well-developed relationship with God and good Bible knowledge as evidenced by a consistent devotional life of Scripture reading and prayer, healthy personal relationships, and a good reputation in her church.

Strong and Steady.
Because the Leader will be a trustworthy ally to those in crisis, she will need to be encouraging and stable, not experiencing serious emotional or psychological problems.

A "People Person"

Because Growing Stronger Groups are all about helping others, the Leader will need to exhibit an authentic love for people and enjoy the caregiving role.

Not a Novice

Because people will more readily accept assistance from someone who "has been there," the Leader should have some life experience in helping others to surmount adversity. While it is not a necessary qualification, if the Leader is also a crisis or trauma survivor, her overcoming example will encourage Participants on their journey.

Accessible

Because caring for people takes time, the Leader will need to commit some time each week to prepare to lead the study and to maintain communication with the Assistant Leader and Pastor. The majority of the Leader's responsibility is at the meeting itself, but she may need to make a mid-week contact or take an occasional phone call from a Participant. For this reason, it is critical that the Leader have a good understanding of boundaries so that she does not feel personally responsible for all the problems of the group. Some Growing Stronger groups have set up a phone tree or confidential online community where group members can support each other during the week.

A Team Player

Because Growing Stronger involves a ministry group, while having strong leadership traits, the Leader must also demonstrate a cooperative, respectful attitude when relating to the Pastor, Assistant Leader, and Counselor.

Reliable

Because women in crisis often experience great insecurity, they need the comfort of knowing that their Growing Stronger Group Leader is reliable and dependable. They need to be able to count on the Leader's consistency in facilitating the group. On rare occasion, if the Leader must miss a meeting, she will need to make arrangements for the Assistant Leader to take her place.

Trustworthy

Because the Leader will be entrusted, by the Participants, with deeply personal information, she must be able to protect the confidentiality of the group. While the Leadership Team provides moral support and consultation for each other, they also must guard the confidentiality of group members. The only exception to this rule is in the case where a Leader has reason to believe that a Participant is an immediate danger to herself or others. In such a situation, the Leader is to call 911 and report the incident to the Pastor and Counselor right away.

STRUCTURING A GROWING STRONGER GROUP

A Growing Stronger Group meets in a home, once a week, for about two hours. The schedule begins with a meal (30 minutes), then a book study (30 minutes), a sharing time (45 minutes), and closes with prayer (15 minutes). The following is a description of the important elements involved.

The Setting

Though Growing Stronger is a ministry of the local church, we find that meeting in a home provides a sense of safety, security, and belonging for the Participants. This may or may not be the Leader's home. The Assistant Leader or someone else may offer to host. Consistency is the key. While there may be occasional exceptions to the rule, meeting in the same home each week will lend a sense of stability to the group. Women in crisis often experience chaos in their own homes, since previous patterns of functioning are not working well at this time. Meeting in someone else's home provides a warm environment for women who may not receive nurturing anywhere else.

The Meal (30 Minutes)

Serving a light meal before the meeting is an important element in Growing Stronger. Eating together helps to establish friendships as a foundation for safe sharing within the group. Starting the meeting with a meal has proven to provide:

- Nurturing. Enjoying a meal (that they don't have to cook!) is very nurturing to women in crisis. Many have been suddenly thrust into the role of single parent/provider and are sorely lacking in nurturing relationships.
- Practical assistance. Many women are coming straight from work to the group.
- Fellowship. Mealtime also provides an opportunity for adult conversation and the chance to catch up with the daily details of each other's lives. Real bonding can happen over a meal.

The Study (30 Minutes)

A book study provides structure for the meeting and gives Participants a healthy focus, bringing relief from the immediate, and potentially all-consuming, crisis. Growing Stronger provides teaching, encouragement, inspiration, and guidelines for surviving and even thriving after a crisis.

Very often crises stem from relational challenges. For this reason, we have included a Curriculum Guide of biblically-based relationship books to follow the Growing Stronger book study. By reading together and sharing about these Christian principles, Participants can process, practice, learn, and implement new relational skills which will protect them from unhealthy situations in the future. Each group member should be prepared to participate in the reading assignments and group discussions for the week.

Sharing Time (45 Minutes)

One of the most important aspects of Growing Stronger groups is the sharing time. Some Participants have expressed that the group is the only place where they can safely talk about their "unspeakable" pain and injury without fear of being judged.

While open sharing is encouraged, boundaries within the group provide a secure environment in which intimacy can grow. It is helpful to establish the following group boundaries from the beginning and gently remind Participants of these boundaries when necessary.

Time boundaries

Establish a pattern of equal time for each person to share. While there may be some weeks when a particular member has an unusual situation requiring a little extra time, generally speaking, try to keep within time boundaries so that everyone gets a chance to share.

Confidentiality

Be sure to stress the importance of each group member respecting the confidentiality of the others. This encourages a sense of safety and intimacy.

Focus

Keep the attention on the week's topic and how it applies to each person's life. This is not a rigid rule, since there will be times when a particular member has an urgent situation to discuss. Generally speaking, however, staying on topic helps maintain the group's direction and fosters individual growth.

Open sharing

Welcome freedom of expression, along with tears and hugs, when appropriate.

Respect

Nonjudgmental listening creates an atmosphere of respect for each person. This may be the only place where some members feel free to openly share.

Unsolicited advice

Encourage group members to avoid giving unsolicited advice. This is a time for Participants to express feelings and thoughts without fear of being judged, lectured, or "fixed." If someone has a response to another's sharing, it is always appropriate to ask first, "May I share something?"

Prayer Time (15 Minutes)

Because James 5:16 says to confess our faults to one another AND pray for one another, Growing Stronger groups make prayer a priority! This is a critical part of caring for each other as, together, we watch God answer prayer. Some women may not have anyone else who is regularly praying for them.

Some groups find it helpful for the Assistant Leader to write down prayer needs of the Participants while the Leader is facilitating the sharing time. This aids organization and saves time gathering prayer requests. The Leader then closes the meeting by praying specifically for each Participant.

A Word about Self-Disclosure

The Growing Stronger group is not the place for the Leader or Assistant Leader to process their own personal issues. However, it can be very helpful for the Leader and Assistant Leader to share with each other and pray for each other's needs during the week. The meeting time is reserved for the group members' needs. Self-disclosure by Leaders can actually hinder the recovery of group members. It can be beneficial, however, for Leaders to share personal victories from the past, or how they previously dealt successfully with a situation similar to that which a Participant shares. Any of the Leader's or Assistant Leader's currently unresolved personal issues should be dealt with outside the group.

The Participants

As was stated earlier, Participants are referred to the Leader by the Pastor, church staff, or church attendee and personally invited by the Leader to join the group.

When to Refer

Sometimes, a potential Participant may present with a situation which is beyond the scope of the Growing Stronger group. In such a case, it is critical to know when and where to refer her to appropriate help. If it becomes apparent that the potential Participant is a danger to herself or others, or if a child or dependent adult is in danger, the Leader must be prepared to call 911 and inform the Pastor immediately. If the Participant is not in a safe situation, it is important for the Leader to consult with the Pastor to see how the church may assist her or refer to those who can. If the client has mental health needs, the Leader can refer her to the Counselor, who will direct her to appropriate services and/or referrals. If the potential Participant is in need of Pastoral ministry or discipleship, the Leader can direct her to the Pastor and a Ladies' Bible study.

When to Invite

After assessing for the above special needs, the Leader may invite the potential Participant to join the Growing Stronger group. Due to the sensitive situations of women in crisis, these groups are intended to function on a continuing, not a drop-in, basis. While not a closed group, it is unsettling to group dynamics if new women are coming and going each week. For this reason, it is recommended that the Leader, who is sensitive to the current group dynamics, explain the nature of the group to the new Participant and personally introduce her at the next group meeting.

It is recommended that groups not exceed eight regularly-attending Participants, as the quality of sharing decreases with larger numbers. Optimal group size is four to six Participants, in addition to the Leader and Assistant Leader. If the need arises, Leaders may choose to start a second group to accommodate increasing numbers.

SMALL GROUP DYNAMICS

A Leader may encounter challenges in group dynamics which require her to resolve tension without alienating group members. The following tips will help guide the Leader in resolving potential problems:

- Keep it real.

    Assure members that it is normal for all groups to undergo some kind of relational challenge.
- Keep your role in mind.

    The Leader's response to conflict resolution provides a healthy role model for group members.
- Keep it in the group.

    Group members are encouraged to first work through minor conflicts between themselves. Conflict in Growing Stronger groups is fairly rare, as members typically become very close by sharing one another's burdens. However, should two members have difficulty resolving a conflict, encourage them not to discuss it among the other members but bring it directly to the Leader for help. If further assistance is needed, the Leader may confer with the Counselor. It is highly unlikely, but if the

Leader and Counselor are not able to help the members settle the issue, they may consult the Pastor to assist in the matter.

- Keep the goal in mind.

    Healthy resolution of conflict promotes respect for each individual, increased intimacy in relationships, and the overall health of the group.

- Keep it general.

    When discussing relational problems in the group, don't allow the problem to bring undue focus on a particular individual; rather, highlight typical challenges in group dynamics.

- Keep it fair.

    As a Leader, remain impartial and exhibit unconditional love and acceptance for each member. Process personal conflicts you may experience with the Counselor so that you can continue to contribute to healthy group dynamics.

- Keep it kind.

    Pace the level of confrontation according to the level of the group's bonding. Secure, mature, grace-filled relationships can handle more confrontation than a newly-formed group. Always speaking the truth in love, remember that grace is the "spoonful of sugar" that helps the medicine of truth to go down!

Personality Types within the Group

All groups experience challenges posed by various personality types. The following are some ideas for working through these common scenarios (Myhre 2002).

When Someone Talks Too Much

There will be occasions when a situation warrants a little extra time for sharing, but when a particular individual habitually talks too much, feelings of awkwardness and even resentment can brew within the group. It is the Leader's responsibility to anticipate and handle this situation so that it does not become a problem.

It is helpful for the Leader to understand why a person may talk too much in a group setting. There may be several reasons for this behavior. She may be narcissistic and think she deserves more than her fair share of time and attention. She may be uncomfortable with periods of silence and feel a sense of responsibility to fill the conversational gap. She may actually use an excessive number of words as a smokescreen to prevent true and intimate sharing. Also, she may simply not understand what is appropriate group sharing and may not know when to stop talking. In any case, the Leader can provide direction to the group by using the following suggestions:

- Be proactive.

  Establish sharing time boundaries early in the group's development to discourage anyone from overtalking.

- Be prompt.

  At the first indication of a problem, take a few minutes during group to go over boundaries and listening skills.

- Be methodical.

  Each week, use the same format to invite people to share. "Who would like to share first tonight? Each person will have a few minutes to share." Determine how many minutes each person will have to share according to the number of people present. At times, a particular member may have an urgent need that will take a little more time. Try to be flexible while remaining aware of the needs of the rest of the group.

- Be prepared.

  Keep the discussion on track by referring to the subject material of the homework. "What does the author have to say about this subject?"

- Be diplomatic.

  Address questions to other people. "I would like to hear what some others have to say about this topic."

- Be discreet.

  Use body language to communicate proper group involvement. Discourage overtalking by avoiding eye contact or other body language responses.

- Be fair.

  Reply, "Thank you for sharing" then move on to another person. A longer response will encourage further overtalking which will, in turn, take away more time from other Participants.

- Be direct.

  If these more subtle responses are not effective, speak with the overly talkative member privately. Kindly inform her of the need for making room for others to share. Show understanding for the reasons she may be overtalking. Inquire how you, as a Leader, can help her with this important group behavior. Realize that by lovingly confronting this member, you are helping her with an issue that is likely affecting her relationships outside of the group as well. Assure her that the group is a safe place to learn new relational skills.

When Someone has Difficulty Sharing

This group member may need encouragement to open up within a group setting. More introverted by nature, this Participant may be observing and learning from others. She will benefit from realizing that others may learn from her too! While it is appropriate for people to quietly contemplate at times, it is the group Leader's responsibility to facilitate, not force, discussion.

With the reluctant talker:

- Be direct.
  Ask for her opinion or how she may feel about the subject at hand.
- Be affirming.
  Affirm her and the value of her contribution to the group discussion.
- Be open.
  Spend a little extra time cultivating a relationship with this member before or after the group. She may need a little more connection to feel secure before disclosing her thoughts to the group.
- Be supportive.
  Offer responsive body language and encouraging, open-ended questions regarding her input to the conversation.

When Someone "Knows it All"

This group member may have difficulty sharing "from the heart" rather than "from the head." In the process, she may unwittingly attempt to offer opinions and unsolicited advice that can cause other members to feel unsafe with the group discussion. She may even come across as being argumentative or judgmental, which can feel threatening to other members. Once again, it is the Leader's job to maintain a safe environment in which everyone, including this member, can feel free to share her personal experiences and needs.

In order to assist this overly-assertive member:

- Be prompt.

  At the very first sign of an argumentative or overly-assertive interaction, don't hesitate to gently interrupt the speaker by saying, "Time out." or "Hold on a minute." then clearly and directly address the situation. Without necessarily singling out one person, speak to the group about the original boundaries by saying something like, "Nonjudgmental listening creates an atmosphere of respect for each person." Then encourage her to ask, "May I share something?" before proceeding, rather than offering unsolicited advice.

- Be unswerving.

  Be prepared to stay on subject by encouraging a member to share how the current topic applies to her own life.

- Be diplomatic.

  Take charge of the tone of the conversation and kindly redirect questions to other people. "I would like to hear what others have to say about this."

- Be firm and kind.

  Remember, you carry the leadership responsibility for the group. Be aware that everyone will be learning from you as you gently, yet decisively, guide this dynamic member who, at some unconscious level, may be testing your leadership. Everyone, including this bold Participant, will feel safe, knowing that you, as a Leader, can speak the truth in love, using your gentle strength to contain the emotional environment of the group. Do be authoritative, understanding that strong leadership is a necessary expression of love which allows the group to function effectively. Don't be authoritarian. Don't allow yourself to be drawn into a power struggle with this member by arguing with her.

- Be clear.

  If the member does not respond to previous measures, explain that talking from an "expert" posture rather than sharing from the heart can cause other group members to feel judged and unsafe.

- Be diligent.

  If overly-assertive behavior persists as problematic, talk privately with the member about how her behavior may be impacting others. If she does not receive correction, she may need to be asked to leave the group.

When Someone Exhibits Control Issues

There may be times when a group member will express a challenge to the authority of the Leader, apparently attempting to struggle for the leadership role of the group. She may habitually interrupt the Leader or other group members or maintain a disagreeable posture. She may view her position as one of helping others, while not addressing her personal issues.

- Be consistent.

  Restate the purpose of the group as outlined in the boundaries, keeping the attention on the week's topic and how it applies to each person's life.

- Be circumspect.

  Remain aware of and avoid control battles. Do not engage in a power struggle. It is a lose/lose situation.

- Be discerning.

  Try to uncover the person's true feelings and needs. Recognize that she may have some "unfinished business" with authority issues that she is acting out in the group. This is a good opportunity for her to learn new ways of relating to authority in a safe setting. If her stated need differs from the group's purpose, refer her to another type of group that better suits her needs.

- Be brave.

   For the health of the group, don't hesitate to talk with this person outside the group in an attempt to determine her core issues.

When Someone is Consistently Overly-Dramatic

Although everyone in the group is there due to a crisis or trauma, a particular type of Participant may exhibit an air of drama, continually calling attention to herself. This can derail the other group members from being able to openly share. Some members with codependent tendencies may be drawn into her unrest and feel responsible to "fix" her. Others may withdraw, overwhelmed by the extreme intensity of her sharing.

In order to maintain healthy group dynamics in such a situation:

- Be observant.

   Watch out for the tendency of other group members who may be inclined to "run to the rescue" of this member. By caretaking in this manner, they can unknowingly enable her learned helplessness, delaying her recovery.

- Be strong.

   As the Leader, don't fall into the codependent trap yourself! While empathizing with the member's concerns, encourage her to be solution-focused and take responsibility for what she can do in the situation.

- Be perceptive.

   Assess the situation. When someone continually "cries wolf," it is possible to not recognize a true emergency when it arises. Although she may express herself in an overly dramatic manner, she may have a real need that deserves the attention of the group.

- Be steady.

  Again, remind the group of the purpose and focus of the meeting, allowing each person equal time.

- Be wise.

  Lovingly distract and redirect rather than openly confront. Encourage members to stay after group to talk if further conversation is needed.

- Be caring.

  One of the best ways to care for any group member is to pray for her! Be sure to schedule the meeting in such a way as to save time at the end for prayer for each person. Knowing that she will receive prayer may relieve some of her underlying fear of not getting the attention she needs.

Lead with Confidence!

Remember that God has put this ministry on your heart and will be faithful to complete the good work which He began in you (Philippians 1:6). He won't let you down, but as you prayerfully lead each week, He will enable and empower you to lead women through recovery to renewed fruitfulness—thirty, sixty, and even a hundred times more than before!

CURRICULUM GUIDE

The following books are recommended reading for group members. These books (to be used after the foundational Growing Stronger book) provide the weekly structure and subject matter for the group. Each book has either a companion workbook or study questions included in the book.

Boundaries: When to Say Yes, When to Say No to Take Control of Your Life, by Dr. Henry Cloud and Dr. John Townsend

Changes That Heal: How to Understand the Past to Ensure a Healthier Future, by Dr. Henry Cloud

Happiness is a Choice, Updated Edition, by Paul Meier, MD and Frank Minirth, MD

He Loves Me! Learning to Live in the Father's Affection, by Wayne Jacobsen

Lord, Heal My Hurts: A Devotional Study on God's Care and Deliverance, by Kay Arthur

Love Is a Choice: The Definitive Book on Letting Go of Unhealthy Relationships, by Dr. Robert Hemfelt, Paul Meier, MD and Frank Minirth, MD.

Safe People: How to Find Relationships That Are Good for You and Avoid Those That Aren't, by Dr. Henry Cloud and Dr. John Townsend

HOW TO FIND A GREAT THERAPIST

By Mary Beth Woll, MA, LMHC

"Wait a second! Find a therapist?!? Do I need therapy? Do we really need it as a couple? With a little willpower, we could handle this on our own, right?"

The truth is, everybody needs counsel, at one time or another, from loved ones, trusted family and friends, pastors, mentors, and professionals. Taking this important step could save a person's life or marriage and potentially change the course of many generations to come!

Before beginning the search for a therapist, it is good to clearly define the need:

- What are my symptoms?
- Is there an immediate threat to someone's safety?
- Is there a desire to include spirituality in therapy?
- Will it be individual, marriage, or family therapy?
- Is there a need for a specialist in treating such cases as Bipolar Disorder, Post-Traumatic Stress Disorder, and others?

- How will I pay for it? Can I use my insurance? (Currently, children are covered under their parent's insurance until age 26, even if married.) Do they offer a sliding scale?
- Would a support group or peer counseling provide what I need or do I need a professional who specializes in my situation?

With all these questions, is it any wonder that many people never make it to the therapist's door? There are good answers to all these questions, but even before answering them, there are often other roadblocks that need to be addressed, like how does one even know when it's time to see a professional?

How can I determine if I need therapy?

Consider when a person catches a cold. If they are sensible, they will drink more fluids and get more rest. If the cold persists, they may take vitamins or over-the-counter cold remedies. If the cold develops into bronchitis or pneumonia, it's time to see a doctor! In such cases, it would be unwise and potentially life-threatening, to continue to self-treat or self-medicate.

In the same way, it is important to recognize when emotional, behavioral, or soul needs are too much for one's personal support system. That's when it's time to stop "white-knuckling it" and get professional help!

As a Christian, shouldn't I just rely on my church and my faith instead of a counselor?

Sometimes a person's faith background or the religious traditions they were brought up with can be a roadblock toward counseling. Many have been taught that if their faith is strong enough, they need not rely on outside counseling. Some wonder, "Is it even O.K. for a Christian to go to therapy? If I were a 'better Christian,' I wouldn't need therapy, right? Shouldn't I just read my Bible and pray more?" This kind of thinking can prolong a person's pain and unnecessarily add to the shame they may already be experiencing. Especially if someone is dealing with past trauma or abuse, some kind of addiction, or any number of other mental health challenges, a trained counselor can be an incredible resource and ally. In these cases, telling them, "You don't need counseling. Just become a better, stronger Christian," or "Just read the Bible and pray more," can condemn them to more years of symptoms, hiding, and unhealthy coping strategies instead of being helpful. In a loving community of faith, we really should be encouraging each other to seek out the help we need, and receiving help from a trained counselor is a wonderful and healthy avenue.

What about medication?

Sometimes, there is a very real and legitimate need for medication in treatment for depression, anxiety, and bipolar disorder, among others. This must not be minimized any more than one would advise a diabetic not to take their insulin! Often people struggle with the idea of starting on medication, thinking that it makes them seem weak or even "crazy." The reality is that the brain is an organ, like any other part of the body, which can become sick. In some cases, the brain is formed a little differently from birth and requires medical support.

Many Christians, and particularly those who have overcome drug addiction, struggle with medication issues, thinking that a "better Christian" would not need an antidepressant or mood stabilizer. This misconception can keep many people away from much-needed treatment. Of course, it is true that God still heals, but apparently, He also chooses to use medicine and does not condemn us for it. Jesus confirmed this when He said in Matthew 9:12, "It is not those who are healthy who need a physician, but those who are sick." Praying for the sick is a vital ministry of the church, but it is just as dangerous for the church to advise against medicine as it would be for pastors and church members to line up and write out prescriptions for each other on Sunday mornings! This calls for a mental health professional.

Although therapists do not prescribe medicine, they can diagnose and refer for proper medical treatment, which is most effective in conjunction with therapy.

Is my past affecting my current life and relationships?

Some people experience childhood sexual abuse or other trauma that is terrifying or impossible for a child to understand. Memories of such horror don't go away. They are so threatening that the mind protects the person by locking these memories away in the subconscious for years while they carry on with the business of growing up. Later, these memories can present as unexplained behavioral symptoms or big blank blocks of time in their childhood memories. When these symptoms begin to emerge in adult years, the person may need someone who can help them articulate and resolve what was previously unspeakable.

When they are ready to face the pain of the past, it is not safe or appropriate to talk to just anyone, although friends and family may play a part in the healing process. It is important that they seek out someone who is trained and skilled in such work; otherwise, it is possible for the unequipped helper to inflict more damage in the process.

How can counseling help my marriage and other relationships?

In addition to depression, anxiety, and post-traumatic symptoms, relationships or marriages may become so conflicted or distant that a third party's perspective and input is needed. Such situations can be overwhelming to a couple's support system of friends and family. Once again, professional help is in order. Seeking counseling, in such cases, is actually the responsible thing to do in order to continue to function well in the family and on the job.

What type of therapist is best for me?

Some of the confusion around finding a great therapist can be resolved by understanding the titles of mental healthcare providers.

- Psychiatrists will usually be identified as "Dr." with "MD" following their name. These medical doctors specialize in the diagnosis and treatment of mental or psychiatric illnesses. They are trained in counseling, but typically use the client's report of symptoms to prescribe appropriate medications and refer clients to therapists for counseling. While it is true that family practice doctors prescribe the overwhelming proportion of antidepressants in the United States, I prefer to recommend a psychiatrist when medication is needed, because, as specialists, they can often catch a subtle need that can make a big difference when prescribing the right medication.

- Psychologists (PhD or PsyD) have a doctoral degree in Psychology. They are specialists in various methods of therapy, as well as psychological testing. Psychologists do not prescribe medications but can refer to a psychiatrist, if necessary.

- Licensed Mental Health Counselors (LMHC, LCPC) have a Master's Degree in Psychology, plus 3,000 hours of post-master's experience in order to be licensed. They are therapists who can diagnose and treat a wide range of problems including depression, anxiety, bipolar disorder, post-traumatic stress disorder (PTSD), sexual abuse, ADD/ADHD, grief, suicidal thoughts, addiction, substance abuse, stress management, self-esteem issues, emotional health, family, parenting and marital issues. In addition to individuals, they can treat couples and families. They do not prescribe medications but can refer to a psychiatrist.

- Licensed Marriage and Family Therapists, (LMFT) are therapists with a Master's Degree in Psychology and post-master's experience (similar to the Licensed Mental Health Counselor) but with more specialized training in issues regarding marriage and family. They can also treat all the issues listed above.

- Licensed Social Workers (MSW, LCSW) also have a Master's Degree in Social Work and post-master's experience. They specialize in providing services to help their clients' psychological and social functioning. Social workers can also treat the above therapy issues. In addition, they are specially trained to provide counseling and resources to help a person better function in their environment and relationships.

- Pastoral Counselors (Rev., M.Div., Pastor) are usually licensed or ordained ministers who also have training in counseling. Their emphasis tends to focus on biblical principles, spiritual formation and direction, and improving relationships. It is important to note that, depending on how or where the Pastor was ordained, they may not have been required to have any training in counseling at all. It is dangerous to assume that all Pastors are equipped to counsel in areas of mental health.

(NOTE: States have similar licenses but may use different license names/initials and may have different requirements. For example, a Licensed Mental Health Counselor (LMHC) in the State of Washington is similar to a Licensed Clinical Professional Counselor (LCPC) in the State of Illinois, but there may be some differences. Don't hesitate to ask for clarification of the initials or degree of a professional when scheduling to see them.)

How can I determine I've found the right therapist for me?

In an effort to answer some of these concerns, I will share how I found my own therapist. Yes, therapists need therapy too! We all have injuries in life. The better healed I am, the better therapist I will be. Experiencing the process also gives me empathy for my clients who are undergoing treatment.

Here are the things that were important to me as I looked for a therapist:

- Covered. She is listed on my insurance plan.
- Competence. She went to a respected university and has a good work history.
- Conviction. There are certain moral principles which are non-negotiable for me. I didn't want to wrestle with these issues during therapy, but needed someone who shared this baseline with me so they would be better able to advise me. Since my faith informs my decisions, choosing a therapist who was also a Christian was THE most important aspect for me.
- Compassion. I found that she is a very caring individual. This is also critical for me. If I felt that the therapist didn't really care, I would go elsewhere.
- Connection. She and I "hit it off." This makes therapy so much more pleasant.
- Consistency. She is dependable and reliable. I know what to expect when I go to therapy.
- Convenience. Her office is within about a half-hour commute. I was willing to travel this distance for a great therapist.

Finding a great therapist has been a huge benefit in my own life. Hopefully, these thoughts will help you navigate the mental healthcare maze to find someone who is a good fit for you. As a counselor, I know that I have the opportunity to change lives daily! Sometimes, like braces, it is slow and incremental. Other times, like heart surgery, it is critical and immediate. Still for others it is like physical therapy—just plain hard work, long-term, and endurance-building.

It takes courage to begin the counseling process. Often, we will experience resistance from within ourselves and from others. This is normal and to be expected. But the rewards are well worth the risk as these life changes can be deep, permanent, and enriching not only for you, but for your loved ones and your marriage. Even one changed life can impact the course of events for generations yet to come!

SUPPLEMENTAL READING FOR GROUP LEADERS

The following books can provide Leaders with further insight in the function and dynamics of small groups.

- How to Lead Small Groups, by Neal McBride
- Lay Counseling, by Dr. Siang-Yang Tan
- Leading Life-Changing Small Groups, by Bill Donahue
- Making Small Groups Work, by Dr. Henry Cloud

BIBLIOGRAPHY

Anne Sullivan Biography. n.d. http://www.biography.com/people/anne-sullivan-9498826#teaching-helen-keller (accessed April 20, 2014).

Arthur, Kay. *Lord, Heal my Hurts: A Devotional Study on God's Care and Deliverance.* Colorado Springs: WaterBrook Press, 2000.

Bunyan, John. *Pilgrim's Progress.* 1628.

Cloud, Dr. Henry. *Changes That Heal: How to Understand Your Past to Ensure a Healthier Future.* Grand Rapids: Zondervan, 1993.

Cloud, Dr. Henry, and Dr. John Townsend. *Boundaries: When To Say Yes, How to Say No To Take Control of Your Life.* Grand Rapids: Zondervan, 1992.

Hammer, Dr. Dan C. *Servant Leadership, A Concept That's Come Into Its Time.* Pacific Creek Books, 2012.

Harriet Tubman Biography. n.d. http://www.biography.com/people/harriet-tubman-9511430 (accessed October 31, 2014).

Helen Keller Biography. n.d. http://www.biography.com/people/helen-keller-9361967#synopsis (accessed April 20, 2014).

Helen Keller Foundation. n.d. http://www.helenkellerfoundation.org/helen-keller/ (accessed April 29, 2014).

Henry, Matthew. *The Blue Letter Bible, Matthew Henry Commentary.* n.d. https://www.blueletterbible.org/Comm/mhc/Rev/Rev_002. cfm (accessed October 31, 2014).

Ilar, Judy. *Facebook.* May 25, 2014. https://www.facebook.com/judy. champion.96?fref=ts (accessed May 25, 2014).

Ilar, Judy. *Facebook.* April 28, 2014. https://www.facebook.com/judy. champion.96?fref=ts (accessed April 29, 2014).

Jacobsen, Wayne. *He Loves Me!: Learning To Live in the Father's Affection. 2nd ed.* Newbury Park: Windblown Media, 2007.

Keller, Helen. *The Story of My Life.* n.d. http://www.afb.org/mylife/ book.asp?ch=P1Ch6 (accessed November 1, 2014).

Liddell, Eric. *The Eric Liddell Centre.* n.d. http://www.ericliddell.org/ ericliddell/home (accessed October 31, 2014).

Lucado, Max. *God Thinks You're Wonderful.* Nashville: Thomas Nelson, 2003.

Meier, MD, Paul D. *The Third Millenium.* Nashville: Thomas Nelson, 1993.

Meier, MD, Paul D.; Hemfelt, Dr. Robert; Minirth, MD, Frank B. *Love Is a Choice.* Nashville: Thomas Nelson, 1989.

Meier, MD, Paul D.; Minirth, MD, Frank B. *Happiness Is a Choice: New Ways to Enhance Joy and Meaning in Your Life.* Grand Rapids: Baker Books, 2013.

Myhre, Kathleen M. . "Discovery Group Teachings at New Life Center." Everett, 2002.

Pottery, Lakeside. *Lakeside Pottery.* n.d. http://lakesidepottery.com/ Pages/kintsugi-repairing-ceramic-with-gold-and-lacquer-better-than-new.htm (accessed May 21, 2014).

Quotes.net, STANDS4 LLC, 2014. "Abraham Lincoln Quotes.". n.d. http://www.quotes.net/authors/Abraham Lincoln (accessed November 1, 2014).

Quotes.net, STANDS4 LLC, 2014. "*Thomas Edison Quotes.*". n.d. http://www.quotes.net/quote/59783 (accessed November 1, 2014).

Tan, Dr. Siang-Yang. *Lay Counseling: Equipping Christians for a Helping Ministry* . Grand Rapids: Zondervan, 1991.

VanderMerwe, Avril. *From Trash to Treasure.* Tomah: Holy Fire Publishing, forthcoming.

Weinberg, Rick. *ESPN 25.* n.d. http://sports.espn.go.com/espn/ espn25/story?page=moments/94 (accessed October 31, 2014).